"Many people wonder, 'How can I live my best life in these uncertain times of change and disruption?' Gail Brenner's book offers practical tools to help you move past feeling stuck in your past or limited by the present. She keeps you company as you learn to find peace of mind to live a fuller life—without changing others—while changing the way you see, and more importantly, *believe* in yourself."

> —**Nance Guilmartin**, author of *Healing Conversations* and *The Power of Pause*

"*Suffering Is Optional* is a must-read for anyone who's ever felt broken or inadequate. Gail offers clear, practical advice, along with tools and practices anyone can implement to find relief from the pain of their own self-judgment. It's possible to see yourself in a whole new light and experience a freer, more peaceful life—and this is the road map to do it."

> —**Lori Deschene**, author of *Tiny Buddha's Gratitude Journal*, and cofounder of the Recreate Your Life Story eCourse

"Truth is always simple. In this profound and easy-to-read book, you will be reminded of what you already know and what has always been with you but has been covered over by your seemingly endless search. Come home and rest in this moment, allowing this book to be a dear friend and a reminder of Truth."

> —**Mary O'Malley**, author of *What's in the Way Is the Way* and *The Gift of Our Compulsions*

"*Suffering Is Optional* points you toward deep, fundamental truths about your true nature and the nature of your experience. It doesn't provide a fix for *what* you experience. It shows you that you are already perfect and whole *regardless* of what you experience. The truths in this book can wake you up to the fact that suffering truly is optional. I will be sharing this one with my own clients and students."

—**Amy Johnson, PhD**, author of *The Little Book of Big Change*, and creator of The Little School of Big Change

"If you are challenged by negative, limiting thoughts or beliefs, self-doubt, anxiety, or fear, this book is for you. Gail Brenner is a gentle, wise, master guide who will lead you on the path of self-love, happiness, and inner peace."

—**Arielle Ford**, author of *Turn Your Mate into Your Soulmate*

"Gail Brenner offers a creative distillation of wise guiding principles and powerful core practices that can free you from your self-induced suffering. Well written and easily accessible, *Suffering Is Optional* points to something that is often completely overlooked in conventional psychological literature—our inherent wholeness and freedom."

—**John J. Prendergast, PhD**, author of *In Touch*; retired adjunct professor of psychology, California Institute of Integral Studies (CIIS)

"At the heart of Buddhism and many forms of modern psychology are two fundamental teachings. The first is that suffering is inevitable. And the second is that suffering can be overcome. For many, this remains an elusive goal, but with Gail Brenner's book, *Suffering Is Optional*, responding to the challenges of life in a new way is not a distant goal, but something that can happen here and now. If you have ever wanted to find a better way, you need look no further than the pages of this book."

—**Darren Main**, author of *Yoga and the Path of the Urban Mystic*

"*Suffering Is Optional* presents what is essentially the most important question of a lifetime: 'If I am not my thought-based identities, then who am I?' With a depth of compassion that can only arise out of honest self-investigation, Gail Brenner clearly lays out how painful and unnecessary thought patterns consistently obscure the effortless fulfillment that is our birthright. Most critically, she presents a practical pathway to permanently cut through tenacious patterns of self-judgment and beliefs in inadequacy. This book is offering you the keys to a life of clarity and freedom. Take the keys and open the door!"

—**Shanti Einolander**, editor of *ONE the Magazine* and
Gangaji's *The Diamond in Your Pocket*

"Gail's book is an amazing combination of direct path invitation into freedom and detailed inquiry into the conditioned thoughts and emotions that obscure it. It shares astute psychological insight and self-help-style writing exercises in a structured way that will benefit both beginners and those already awake to their true nature. Its clarity and compassionate wisdom are a beautiful and inspiring expression of Being, showing the reader the 'sacred return home.' I learned a few shortcuts home myself, thanks to Gail!"

—**Grace Bubeck, PhD**, therapist, meditation teacher, spiritual
mentor, and founder of Living from Love live online events

# SUFFERING IS OPTIONAL

## A SPIRITUAL GUIDE TO FREEDOM FROM SELF-JUDGMENT & FEELINGS OF INADEQUACY

## GAIL BRENNER, PhD

NEW HARBINGER PUBLICATIONS, INC.

# Publisher's Note

*This publication is designed to provide accurate and authoritative information in regard to the subject matter covered. It is sold with the understanding that the publisher is not engaged in rendering psychological, financial, legal, or other professional services. If expert assistance or counseling is needed, the services of a competent professional should be sought.*

Distributed in Canada by Raincoast Books

Copyright © 2018 by Gail Brenner
Reveal Press
An imprint of New Harbinger Publications, Inc.
5674 Shattuck Avenue
Oakland, CA 94609
www.newharbinger.com

Cover design by Amy Shoup

Acquired by Katie Parr

Edited by Ken Knabb

All Rights Reserved

FSC
www.fsc.org
MIX
Paper from
responsible sources
FSC® C011935

RAINFOREST ALLIANCE
CERTIFIED

## Library of Congress Cataloging-in-Publication Data

Names: Brenner, Gail F., author.
Title: Suffering is optional : a spiritual guide to freedom from self-judgment and
    feelings of inadequacy / Gail Brenner, PhD.
Description: Oakland, CA : New Harbinger Publications, Inc., [2018] | Includes
    bibliographical references. |
Identifiers: LCCN 2017055011 (print) | LCCN 2017058807 (ebook) | ISBN
    9781684030163 (PDF e-book) | ISBN 9781684030170 (ePub) | ISBN
    9781684030156 (pbk. : alk. paper)
Subjects: LCSH: Suffering. | Self-perception. | Spiritual life.
Classification: LCC BF789.S8 (ebook) | LCC BF789.S8 B75 2018 (print) | DDC
    204/.42--dc23
LC record available at https://lccn.loc.gov/2017055011

20    19    18

10    9    8    7    6    5    4    3    2    1        First Printing

*You are infinitely free,*
*unendingly magnificent,*
*undeterred by fear,*
*overflowing as love itself.*


*This is your true nature,*
*alive in you in this very moment.*

# CONTENTS

# FOREWORD

I was born four years after World War II to a father who suffered from severe PTSD, epilepsy, and alcoholism, but who was nonetheless a sensitive, gifted professional artist. My mother bore the brunt of his obscenity-laden drunken rages (which we kids listened to throughout many long nights). She eventually attempted suicide three times and spent most of my adolescence in psychiatric institutions.

I dropped out of high school after a year of drug use, for which I was arrested twice. Most people throughout history have had it much worse.

Suffering seems endemic to life. The struggle to overcome it and achieve happiness defines the human endeavor. Gail Brenner is not the first to make the bold claim that "suffering is optional." The founders of most spiritual traditions proclaimed that they had found a way out of suffering and were experiencing "the Kingdom of Heaven within", Nirvana, Samadhi, etc. Moreover, they offered teachings and practices through which their followers might do the same.

I reached my nadir one summer evening in 1968. I'll spare you the details, but I resolved to stop taking drugs and learn to meditate.

I kept that resolution, and have been meditating at least an hour a day, without fail, ever since. In 2009, I started *Buddha at the Gas Pump*: a YouTube channel and podcast featuring conversations with "ordinary" spiritually awakening people. It is the most successful show in its genre. I met and interviewed Gail Brenner at the Science and Nonduality Conference, at which she and I and many people I've interviewed attend and speak annually. While interviewing her, it was evident that she is adept at weaving together nondual understanding with traditional psychology.

As you'll see in this book, Gail understands the psychology behind feeling unworthy and inadequate, and, as many first-person accounts attest, she is able to help people discover that our true nature is not unworthy and inadequate. This renders suffering optional, and opens the possibility of discovering happiness in any moment. Gail has a gift for expressing spiritual truths in common language that anyone can understand. Her commonsense approach doesn't attempt to improve the story but gets to the heart of the problem—our mistaken identity.

Although the mechanics of the practice I learned are different from what Gail presents in this book, the essential principle is the same. As she puts it, "You are infinitely free, unendingly magnificent, undeterred by fear, overflowing as love itself. This is your true nature, alive in you in this very moment." If she and all the world's wisdom traditions are right, suffering shouldn't afflict us any more than thirst should afflict fish. If, that is, we can evoke and stabilize the experience of our "true nature." This book offers to help you do that.

I'm a big fan of methodical approaches to personal and spiritual development. Listening to talks, reading books, and watching YouTube videos can make us intellectually top-heavy if we don't counterbalance understanding with direct experience. In this book, Gail also offers five core practices for "using practical means to move out of the rut of reactivity and respond in new ways." Having attuned to our "true nature," we may still experience failures, diseases, divorce, and all of life's challenges, but they will be buffered by an inner reserve of fulfillment.

Those who experience themselves as limited, broken, and inadequate, and who experience life as meaningless and difficult, are like lottery winners who don't realize they've won—whose winning ticket lies forgotten in a sock drawer while they struggle to get by. In fact, everyone on earth is a lottery winner. We all possess the innate capacity to live happy, meaningful lives. If enough of us tap and utilize that capacity, we'll transform the world! May this book add significantly to our numbers.

—Rick Archer
Host of *Buddha at the Gas Pump*

# GETTING STARTED

"I feel like a loser." These were the words of my friend Natalie, as we were sitting over coffee, and they just didn't compute. Before me I saw a beautiful woman who is gifted in so many ways. But every time she expressed clarity or excitement about her life's direction, in a split second her thoughts derailed her. "I can't…" "It won't work…" No wonder she felt like a loser. Her thoughts were constantly telling her lies that she took to be true. As I listened to her story, I was struck by the impressive power of the thinking mind.

Whether we call it being a loser, hating ourselves, or feeling damaged, inadequate, or unworthy, it breaks my heart to realize how many of us live under this cloud of painful thinking. We long for ease within ourselves and in our relationships. We're filled with dreams and creative ideas just itching to be expressed in the world. Then these negative beliefs roll in like a tornado, convincing us that we're not good enough, squashing our dreams, and keeping us constantly on edge. If you're like I was many years ago, you're probably asking, "Is this all life has to offer? Am I doomed to struggle forever?" Are you truly undeserving of happiness, peace, and the simple enjoyment of a life well lived?

We live in a culture of inadequacy. We hear messages everywhere telling us that we should do more, be more, have more, and endlessly improve ourselves. And the experiences many of us carry from our families have led us to conclude that we're insufficient and lacking what we need to be whole. These deeply felt influences breed a mind-set of wishful thinking: "If only I were more confident and less afraid… If only my life story had been different…" And we're left feeling alienated and bereft, trying with good intentions to find our way to peace and happiness, but not quite getting there.

Yet we keep searching, which speaks to the tremendous resilience of the human spirit. Buried within us is a seed of knowing that we are so much greater than our imagined limits. And this knowing tells us that the desire to search for a way out of this suffering can be trusted. Why? *Because it is not your birthright to feel inadequate.* Your essence is and always has been whole, loving, completely peaceful, primed for joy, and lacking nothing. It's your natural state—available right now—and knowing this is where freedom lies.

But this truth is usually overlooked. If you're reading this book, you have probably been captured by your thoughts and emotions, taking them to be a true reflection of reality. You believe you're a victim, a loser, or a damaged person who is unable to control your emotions. You view the world through these filters that don't serve your happiness and well-being.

With this familiar layer of confusing thoughts and feelings firmly in place, how do you find your way back to your true home of wholeness and peace? How do you navigate through the pain to experience your natural expression of joy and enthusiasm? How do you stop seeing yourself—and the world—as your enemy or your savior?

## Nondual Understanding—What Sets You Free

I have studied this problem inside and out and have found only one solution. And the path to this solution is to explore life's most essential question: Who are you? If you believe yourself to be inadequate, or if you think you're undeserving of satisfying relationships and a fulfilling life, then you are taking yourself to be something you're not. You've convinced yourself that you don't matter or that you're too broken to thrive.

*But these limiting and painful identities you hold about yourself just aren't true.* They're made up of familiar and conditioned thoughts and feelings, but they don't accurately describe who you are.

If you are not these thought-based identities, then who are you?

The approach in this book is an expression of ancient and contemporary nondual teachings, which get to the facts about what is false and what is real. This approach is radical because it invites us to question all of our assumptions. Everything we take to be true is the subject of our investigation. We don't assume that your ideas about yourself are real just because you believe them. We want to know what is *absolutely* real. Why believe something about yourself that isn't true—especially if it brings so much pain to your life? Are you really broken and inadequate? Here we don't assume that the answer is yes, so we can examine this crucial question with the eyes of truth.

The word "nondual" means "not two." The invitation of nonduality is to explore beyond your mind and emotions and beyond the personal self that you think you are. And we'll do that by unraveling the identity you cling to: that you are deficient, inadequate, and not good enough. We'll dissect this identity so carefully that in the end you'll know in your heart of hearts that it just isn't true.

What you'll discover is an amazing fact. No matter what you *think* about yourself and how badly you feel, there is something else going on. There is *always* a part of your experience that is aware, alive—and problem-free. But don't take my word for it. Check in with yourself right now. Are you aware? Are you conscious and alive? Of course you are! And knowing this is the exciting beginning of finding freedom from the limiting belief that you're unworthy.

In any moment, you can suffer—or you can be free. You can be embroiled in the story about believing you're unworthy—or you can be fully engaged in your present-moment experience, where you're breathing, seeing, hearing, walking, speaking. You're simply here, aware, living this moment. In our journey together, we'll return over and over to this experience of being aware in the present moment. As you do that, you're leaving behind the limited identity that you've always thought defined you. Over time, it begins to lose its power, and you'll eventually get a taste of the freedom that's possible beyond it.

What's so great about being aware in the present moment? This being-aware experience is free of all mind activity. When your attention is here in presence, you're not tangled up in unhappy thoughts, so you're peaceful, open, and at ease. You naturally feel connected to yourself, and, in an indefinable way, you feel connected to everything else as well. You're in harmony with all of life. It's here where you'll find that sense of wholeness that you so desperately want. It's already who you are—you've just been too distracted to realize it.

This fresh way of being is not just for enlightened sages or monks living on mountaintops. The nondual nature of reality is the essence of all present-moment experience, which means it is practical, real, and alive in you right now. Freedom from the limiting identity that you're unworthy is available in any moment. The path is direct: you realize the false beliefs that have taken hold and you open to the possibility of returning your attention to being aware now. Then you're able to fully live, unveiled and overflowing with life-giving potential.

## Untangling Inadequacy

As humans, though, the problem we call personal inadequacy or unworthiness seems very real—and painful. You feel hurt, rejected, disappointed, or ignored, and since these everyday experiences stick to you like glue, they need to be addressed. This book offers trusted tools and wisdom-based insights to help you untangle these identities. As you bring them to your present moment experience, you're more available to the spaciousness of your true nature that is free of mental and emotional entanglements. Simply said, you suffer less.

These negative identities we hold about ourselves are a product of the thinking mind, and the mind is a formidable power that doesn't let go easily. In my work as a therapist, I've seen many people cling to the belief that they are damaged and broken, playing it out in their daily lives with painful results. The patterns we're speaking about here are very entrenched. You've come to believe these false ideas about yourself probably from early on in childhood, so the roots run deep.

The good news is that your personal story of unworthiness and even self-hate *can* be untangled, because it's built on confused thinking and it's not the essence of who you are. You *can* know the endless peace you long for.

If discovering this truth sounds challenging, don't worry, because you don't have to go it alone. I'll walk with you as your eyes open to understand how you've come to believe you're unworthy. We'll carefully investigate how the belief in personal inadequacy makes you suffer, and, like scientists, we'll examine any ideas you hold about yourself, other people, and the world to see if they are distorted or true. And I'll be your most enthusiastic companion as the fog of unworthiness starts to clear and you become familiar with the natural, unconditioned state of ease and well-being.

By the time you finish this book, you'll be able to recognize all the ways that self-defeating thoughts creep in, and you'll have the confidence that you can apply the resources needed in the moment to lift the veil of personal inadequacy and find your way back to clarity and sanity.

## Discovering Freedom in My Own Experience

How do I know all this? What I'm presenting here for you is exactly the path that I have already traveled. I had been locked into fear and self-doubt for decades, searching for a way to be fully myself both inside and out without that nagging voice telling me I wasn't okay. For years I worked with lovely, well-intentioned therapists who tried to help me develop a better perspective of myself and the events from my past, but somehow I didn't feel any better.

Things began to shift once I discovered the value of being present. Instead of looking for a way to improve my personal story, I learned to do something radically different, which was to become aware of the elements of my in-the-moment experience. I was initially shocked to notice the array of painful and disruptive thoughts that occupied my mental space, and I realized that many agitated feelings were rumbling around in me, mostly outside of conscious awareness.

With the guidance of wonderful teachers, I spent hours, days, and sometimes weeks in meditation being a witness of these experiences. And in doing that, something magical happened. These thoughts and feelings became less important, and some of them disappeared forever. I remember standing in the middle of the vast high desert in southern California one afternoon during a meditation retreat. It seemed like lifetimes of ancient resentments were being released from my body and mind and carried away by the wind.

I returned to my everyday life feeling lighter and so much more surrendered, but I knew my journey wasn't finished. Just being aware of the rising and passing away of thoughts, feelings, and sense perceptions, what we call mindfulness, still left me with burning questions about how to be free of suffering.

I became fascinated by spiritual teachings of nonduality that point beyond thinking to pure aware presence as the fundamental source of everything, the ever-present ground of being. My path took me deeper into questions about identity, to know what was real beyond the false belief that I was a separate personal self. I started asking the essential spiritual question: Who am I?

I noticed that just about any time I was lost in thought, I was thinking negative ideas about myself, other people, situations, the past, or the future. When I was gripped by these thoughts, I felt anxious and unhappy, and my body was filled with tension. One sunny day, I was lying outside on a lounge chair enjoying the peace and quiet. It came to me to experiment with thought and no thought. Every time I started thinking about something, I felt my body contract. And when I withdrew my attention from the thought to simply be present, I relaxed. I went back and forth a few times, and it became so apparent to me that engaging with thoughts created agitation and letting them go brought peace.

Taking this insight into my daily life, the more I became disinterested in thoughts—any thoughts—the happier I was. If I didn't give thoughts power by thinking about them and believing their content, I wasn't listening to their limitations, criticisms, worries, and pronouncements about what other people should say or do. And I felt way more connected to everyone and everything.

Just like a snake sheds its skin, I shed limiting personal identities and beliefs that were behind my fears. And the shedding revealed wide-open space, clarity about people and situations, a flow of creativity, and a quiet, still presence that is the source of life itself. There are no problems here—no inadequate me, no fear, no painful past, and no self-doubt. This restful space is what's always here and available, at the core of every moment, and it's discovered once the attachment to thinking dissolves.

You can think of this process as the sacred return—shifting from entrapment in the mind's belief systems to presence and peace.

## The Offering to You

I was excited to bring this new understanding of identity to my work as a psychotherapist. I saw that just about every problem clients came in with could be boiled down to identifying with thoughts that just weren't true. I began to experiment with ways to meet people where they are—in their belief of these distorted thoughts about themselves and the stories that give rise to them—and then guide them to see that freedom is always possible.

This book is built on the revolutionary idea that the suffering you experience from feeling unworthy is optional. You don't *have to* believe thoughts that tell you you're inadequate. I come to this work with great enthusiasm because I absolutely know that behind the veil of any personal problem you think you have is the aliveness of your true nature. This underlying fabric of reality is untouched by past experiences, thoughts, or emotions, and it's right here—now and always.

When you know this reality, your relationship to your thoughts, your feelings, and the situations that arise in life changes completely. Your attention is no longer trapped in your own limiting story, so you're free to be attuned to what's happening now. You meet your own challenging experiences with loving compassion. You're present with others and knowingly alive in the moment. You're naturally openhearted and you see situations with fresh eyes. No longer needing to protect or defend yourself, you're fully available to life. Can you feel the freedom? I'm thrilled to bring this possibility to you.

Since you've been living in the stew of believing you're insufficient and undeserving, you might feel hopeless about the potential for new insights. Maybe you've tried many means—workshops, self-help books, psychotherapy—and still don't feel better. And you're left wondering why engaging wholeheartedly in this approach will be any different.

I'm inviting you to suspend your doubts enough so you can begin to question the truth of your thoughts. Although you may not realize it, you've been consumed by thinking about yourself in ways that just aren't true. I encourage you to consider saying "Enough!" to the suffering and to offer a full-on "Yes!" to what's actually possible for you. That's what I did years ago when I became completely fired up to untangle myself from false ideas and know the truth. I had had enough of suffering. I was willing to put every treasured belief in the fire, to let it burn and see what remained. And with time and consistent practice, I began to experience the effortless way of presence, the peace that comes from knowing you're not separate from life, and the clear seeing that allows you to navigate even sticky situations in life.

If this intimacy with life is possible for me, I know that it's possible for you. You are not whatever your thoughts might tell you that you are. You, in your essence, are whole, strong, tender, awake, and infinitely free.

## How to Use This Book

This book is arranged in two parts. In the first part, "Laying the Groundwork," I'll introduce the four guiding principles and five core practices that are the foundation of this approach to the problem of feeling broken and inadequate. The guiding principles bring you through the fog of distorted thinking about yourself to anchor you in what is absolutely true. The practices show you how to be free of this problem. They can be applied in any moment, no matter what you're experiencing, and by using them over and over you'll be primed to discover that the peace of your true nature is right here at the heart of any experience.

How do you live when you're free of the torment of inadequate thinking? The second part, "Living Free," relates these principles and practices to three specific aspects of the problem of personal inadequacy. We'll cover ways to have a better relationship with your past; the mind-set needed to no longer take things personally; and living from love and openness and not fear.

I recommend that you read Part 1 so as to establish a strong foundation. Then move on to the specific topics in Part 2 that you think will benefit you the most.

Just reading about this exciting possibility of being free of the identity of lack and inadequacy is not nearly enough. You need to actively participate. Throughout the book, I've included exercises, experiments, and reflections, and I encourage you to work with them so you can untangle your own limiting identities. The more you engage with the ideas presented here, the more you'll melt into the truth of who you are. You'll get to know, without a doubt, that you are not the pained and diminished one your thoughts tell you that you are.

For your convenience, I've prepared a downloadable workbook containing all the activities suggested in the book, which you can access at http:www.newharbinger.com/40156 (see the very back of this book for more details). In addition, at that same web page you'll find two guided audio meditations. In the first one, I guide you through the five core practices; the second offers a short reset for coming home to yourself when you're lost in feelings of inadequacy and self-judgment.

This book also includes stories from clients, other people I've known, and my own experience to give you real-world examples of how the principles and practices work. All identifying information except my own has been changed to protect confidentiality. I hope these examples show you that you don't have to be special to be relaxed, complete, and whole as life unfolds. It is absolutely possible for you in your own life experience.

I know the pain of feeling inadequate, of worrying that you're messing up, and of longing for love that you think you're missing. But I also know without a doubt that these are fleeting and limiting ideas that mask the truth of luminous presence and unbounded aliveness. You, too, can be free of these limiting ideas and know your brilliance beyond them. So let's get started…

# PART 1

# LAYING THE GROUNDWORK

# CHAPTER 1

# DISCOVERING FREEDOM

> Don't expect anything and you get everything.
>
> —Jean Klein

Believing that you're damaged or inadequate is a powerful identity that contains a great deal of momentum. It's a story of lack that you've lived by for probably most of your life. It tells you that you don't matter, that you're not lovable, and that you need to define yourself by how others see you.

My client Joe had a rough start in life. He lived in a series of foster homes until he was adopted into a loving family at age five. Joe is blessed with a great sense of humor and is one of the funniest people I've ever known. It's a gift that served him well during his childhood, but as an adult he feels a tremendous pressure to entertain whoever he is with and can't relax unless he keeps them laughing.

Can you feel into what he experiences? Joe is empty and bereft inside, and he avoids these painful feelings by constantly scanning for other people's reactions. He feels a few moments of safety only when he can be sure they think he's funny. It's exhausting for his inner sense of peace to be completely dependent on the reactions of others, and his peace is fleeting.

## The Value of Suffering

When you begin working with this identity of unworthiness, it might feel like you're on a freight train barreling down the tracks that you can't control. This way of defining yourself grabs you and doesn't let go. The identity seems so real and your reactions seem so familiar that you assume they're true without questioning them.

When you're immersed in these beliefs of inadequacy and brokenness, you live the precious moments of your life, including this one happening right now, completely unaware of the possibility of shedding these misconceptions about yourself. Steeped in self-doubt and gripped by thoughts that keep you disappointed and disillusioned, it doesn't even seem like an option to consciously step into your life and live from the fullness of your being. Most of us have no insight into the truth of the matter—that the happiness we long for is actually here and available right now. And even if that sounds like a good idea, we have no clue about how to find it in our own experience.

But the fact that you're suffering is your wake-up call. In those moments of honest self-reflection, when you admit that things aren't working for you the way they are, you stop avoiding your experience and you open to the pain of what you're actually feeling—the sorrow, frustration, alienation, and longing. These are moments of grace, when the wall of the conditioned pattern cracks just enough for you to contemplate possibilities outside your known reality. *Suffering calls you into deeper questions about who you are.*

When I'm working with a client who courageously turns toward her experience and feels pain, maybe for the first time, inside I'm secretly rejoicing. I have tremendous compassion for what she's feeling, but I know that she has begun the journey from darkness to the light of full conscious living. If she is willing to meet the pain directly and understand how it affects her so strongly, she's on the road to realizing that the personal identity she has held about herself is false. She'll discover what lies beyond the pain—the innocence of the truth of who she is, which is expansive, overflowing with life, and unlimited by the messages she has received about herself from her interactions with others.

Becoming aware of what you're experiencing in any moment is the key to interrupting the momentum of this conditioned identity. Because *now* is the only time you have a choice. If you withdraw your attention from limiting thoughts, you're doing that now. If you relate differently to the emotions you feel, that is happening now. And if the personal identity falls apart to reveal your glorious true nature, it happens in the timeless now.

The mind takes you away into the past and future, which is why you suffer. It pulls you into believing judgments and expectations that don't serve peace and happiness. And being lost in the mind is the fuel for these misguided patterns to run wild.

Bringing awareness to the thoughts and feelings that are the objects of suffering, and opening into being present right now, gives you a glimpse of reality beyond these mind-made limits. Once these insights emerge about the truth of things, identifying as inadequate just won't make sense anymore. You'll see it as old news, a made-up role that doesn't touch your true magnificence.

When you know that suffering is a valid part of your journey, you use the situations and emotions that appear in order to awaken from the trance of inadequacy, rather than taking them as your unsatisfying reality.

This is a radically new way of being with your experience, so walking this path requires support. The support I offer here is based on four guiding principles and five core practices. In nondual teachings of what is called the direct path, there is actually only one practice, which is to continually return your attention to the boundless space of awareness. These core teachings point only to this one absolute reality—the pure aliveness that is always here at the heart of any object or experience.

Ultimately, resting attention in this space of awareness is where you'll find release from the suffering of believing you're a separate person who is inadequate. But my work over the years has shown me that additional skillful means are often needed. The human mind can be a force to reckon with as it clings to personal stories. The feelings we experience seem so real, and we play out reactive patterns even though they keep us anxious and disturbed.

So here I present four guiding principles and five core practices. The guiding principles point you to what's real beyond any limiting ideas about yourself, and they are available to support you when you're caught in programmed habits of thinking. The core practices will help you untangle the personal identities you believe are true, paving the way to consciously realize your true nature, which is already peaceful and at ease.

These principles and practices will be discussed in detail throughout the book, and you'll learn exactly how to use and apply them. When you've sunk into a hole and can't seem to find your way out, you can draw on the principles to understand why you're suffering and engage with the practices to shift your in-the-moment experience. Then you're carrying out your only job—to meet what appears with insight, understanding, and loving acceptance.

## Four Guiding Principles

The four guiding principles remind you of what's true when you're caught in the false idea that something is wrong with you. If your mind is preoccupied with thoughts of inadequacy, you're distracted from being present and you're not at peace. Standing in these principles will loosen the grip of limiting beliefs you hold about yourself.

## How Conditioning Works

The first two guiding principles describe the nature of conditioned identities that are at the root of your suffering. I invite you to take out the microscope and begin to study your experience so you can understand exactly how you end up believing that you're broken and lacking.

1.  The identity of "I am not enough" is made up of distorted thoughts that view the self, others, and the world through a lens that is limited and false.

2.  No matter how real it seems, the identity of unworthiness is optional. You don't *have to* be defined by it.

In the next chapter, we'll look in great detail at the process by which identities take hold, but for now here's an overview of why the first two guiding principles are so integral to finding freedom from your stories of personal inadequacy.

Conditioned ways of thinking develop over time from the conclusions you drew about yourself from your past experiences. If you don't question these beliefs, you assume they're true and they become the veil through which you live in the world. The problem with conditioned thinking patterns is that they make you believe you're something you're not. This view of things seems so real!

When you're grabbed by conditioning, you're not conscious of the full reality of the present moment. You're asleep to what is actually happening right now. Smokers trying to quit will tell you that they suddenly realize they're in the middle of smoking a cigarette. They've actually picked up the cigarette, lit it, and started smoking, but these actions happened outside of conscious awareness.

How much of your life is passing you by while you're going through the motions like a robot, mindlessly playing out unquestioned beliefs about yourself? Unless you're awake and aware as life unfolds, you're in the tunnel of conditioning and you're missing out on the magnificence of actually living this human life. Something in you just knows this way of conditioning can't be all there is. We can't be here only to muddle our way through, battling our inner demons.

There is, however, a strong motivation to avoid exploring our inner experience. When you put the brakes on the momentum of conditioning and stop hiding from your feelings, you open to everything—and some of what you discover may be challenging. You become aware of painful feelings you've been avoiding and the strategies you've been using to distract yourself from them. When you have an inkling of difficult emotions underneath the surface, if you're like most people you go into your head, get busy, use substances, focus on getting your needs met by the world and other people—anything but actually stopping and feeling the feelings.

Part of your journey to realizing your essential wholeness involves shining the light of conscious awareness onto all aspects of your programmed habits. You study these habits to discover that they are made up of distorted thoughts that confuse your view of reality. You welcome feelings, embracing them with the deepest acceptance. And you come to realize that believing this identity of inadequacy is optional. You don't *have to* believe that you're worthless and unlovable. You don't *have to* live feeling empty and sad. It's not your birthright to constantly be seeking validation from others. You consciously realize that you're suffering, so you can find your way out of the suffering.

## *Waking Up to Your Experience*

The third and fourth guiding principles help remind you to look beyond your thoughts and feelings to discover the peace that's here at the heart of every moment.

3.  You have control over shifting your attention to different parts of your experience.

4. There is more to your experience in any moment than your thoughts and feelings.

As we move forward, we'll focus a lot on where you place your attention and how that affects you. When your attention is stuck in painful thoughts and feelings, the world will feel like one big disappointment. But you'll be amazed to realize that you have control over where you place your attention.

You'll learn the tools to withdraw your attention from the belief systems that don't serve your happiness. And rather than being lost in feeling badly, you'll discover that you can meet your feelings with clarity and love. As you break down the elements of the identity that used to trouble you, you realize that you now have a whole new relationship with your thoughts and feelings. The habitual cyclone of suffering starts to lose its grip so you're available to explore your experience beyond it.

What is beyond your thoughts and feelings? This is the treasure waiting to be discovered that frees you from the trap of limiting beliefs about yourself. When the veil of the personal self falls away, with all its fears and imperfections, you realize that who you are is not the one with the familiar story of suffering. With no story defining you, you're expansive, boundless, and free. You welcome life as it is right now—not how you expect it or want it to be, but how it actually is. The inner war with your experience ends as peace pervades.

## Five Core Practices

The four guiding principles offer insights into the reality of your experience—how it actually is and not what the false thinking of the separate self makes you believe it is. The five core practices are the breadcrumbs that show you the way home to peace. Each will be covered in a separate chapter so you'll know exactly how and when to use them.

You'll come to trust the art and craft of acknowledging your inner experience and deploying the best resources to support your path to freedom. Even when you discover painful feelings or harsh judgments in the mind, you'll be able to take a deep breath, gather yourself, and open up to what's present with intelligence and grace.

If you continue to avoid your in-the-moment experience, your attention will stay out in the world trying to get your needs met and you'll inevitably be disappointed. People and situations will never be reliable sources of the inner wholeness you long for. Where do you find that inner wholeness? At the risk of stating the obvious, you need to look within. And these practices will support you, over and over, as you do just that.

## Core Practice #1: *Turning Toward Your Experience*

As humans, we're programmed to seek comfort and avoid pain. Our attention goes everywhere to distract us from what we're actually experiencing. We need a radical shake-up to see past these long-standing, limiting habits. Knowledge is crucial.

You need to become the world's best expert on how you get caught, so you can spot when these patterns take hold. You'll get to know intimately how these painful identities live in you—how they feel in your body, the thoughts that support them, the emotions that keep them alive, and the ways they make you behave in the world that are based on fear and need. You start by turning your attention toward the inner landscape of what you're experiencing.

## Core Practice #2: *The Safe Haven of Being Aware*

As you turn toward your experience, you become aware of exactly what's happening within you. Pressing "pause" on the momentum of conditioning, you withdraw your attention from being involved with the stories of suffering, and you notice the thoughts, say hello to the feelings, recognize the constriction in your breathing and other body sensations, and feel the urges to act.

Then you explore this experience of being aware itself. And you realize it's always here as your reliable safe haven, closer than the breath. It's the field of awareness that is always at peace no matter what thoughts and feelings appear.

## Core Practice #3: *Losing Interest in Thoughts*

Believing the content of your thoughts creates suffering. With a willingness to explore everything, you'll study the language thought uses, the inner critical voice that plays in your head, and the nature of thinking itself. You'll be able to identify judgments, comparisons, stories, and other thoughts that bring about suffering. And you'll feel the relief of losing interest in the content of thoughts fueled by fear and separation.

## Core Practice #4: *Welcoming Feelings*

Turning toward feelings reveals how they live in your body. And welcoming the physical sensations is the gateway to presence. The story *about* the feelings takes your attention away from the here and now. Even though it sounds paradoxical, when you deeply allow feelings to be present without resisting them, you'll discover freedom from the pain.

## Core Practice #5: *The Sacred Return*

The sacred return is not a practice like the first four that you apply to the belief that you're unworthy and lacking. It's what is revealed once you see clearly that the painful thoughts and feelings don't actually define you. You realize that you're not the limited, separate person who is doomed to live forever with a hole inside that can't be filled up. As this idea is seen through, your attention returns to your true home where you're simply aware. Thoughts and feelings appear, but they're seen as part of the whole and lose their power to disturb you. You leave the world of false beliefs and rest in this pure, welcoming presence, the boundless peace of who you are. Then you reenter the world with clarity and insight, and you are moved by love, not lack.

## Support from the Core Principles and Practices

These principles and practices work beautifully together to support you in beginning to live from the wholeness that you are. The four guiding principles bring crystal clear understanding to your experience in the moment so you perceive what's going on with truth and authenticity. The five core practices set the stage for using practical means to move out of the rut of reactivity and respond in new ways. Together, they set in motion a course of loving care for yourself and your experience that changes everything. A new beginning is right here and available for you, and it starts in every moment.

Here's how it works. Once you realize you're caught in a whirl of negative thinking, you take a conscious breath. Already, the light of awareness shines as you're less entangled in your thoughts. Turning toward your experience, you're now aware of your inner world of thoughts, emotions, and bodily sensations, so you can see what is actually happening that is making you suffer.

Losing interest in the content of thoughts and embracing the sensations in your body, you begin to explore something wondrous, which is the calm and peaceful space of being aware. It's here as the background of every moment, outside the realm of the mind—still, open, and vibrating with aliveness.

Settling your attention in this being-aware space, you have a completely different relationship with the conditioned identity of unworthiness. Seeing the fullness of the moment as it really is—and not in the tunnel vision of the identity—it dawns on you that these distorted thoughts don't define you and that believing them is truly optional. This programming will grab you again and again, but each time you notice it you welcome it with clarity and compassion, and let it be.

When you're captured by thought patterns of inadequacy, you're believing a constructed reality that will never leave you feeling fulfilled. It's like walking through a dark and narrow tunnel with no light at the end and no acknowledgment that a whole world of possibility exists outside the tunnel. Maybe this is how you live a good part of the time.

You know by now how your mind will lead you. It's the nature of the mind to doubt and nitpick. And trying to change the mind to think positively is a herculean task that doesn't offer you a sustainable, practical way of returning to peace and happiness. If you believe what it tells you, you're left feeling empty, hopeless, and despairing. And you know what that looks like:

- You find yourself in relationships in which others take advantage of you.

- You're scared to share your ideas in a meeting.

- You're sensitive to taking things personally.

- You run yourself ragged trying to get approval from others.

- You're afraid of your own brilliance.

These stressful moments of disconnection need care, understanding, and new ways of responding, which is what the guiding principles and core practices provide.

Applying them, you're no longer self-focused, constantly feeling a sense of lack and trying to figure out how to fill it up. As you move beyond personal ideas about yourself, you discover space to be in touch with the real-life possibility of being generous, open, and free as you live in the world. You realize that nothing about you needs to be fixed, healed, made better, or improved. You're connected to presence and available to new, uplifting, and authentic ways of being.

It will take some practice, but the sacred return to your true nature is possible for you. When you understand how these painful beliefs grab you and when you know the helpful actions to make, it takes just a few seconds to find your way to peace. And each time you do this, the habit of inadequate thinking that's been plaguing you for years softens.

Ultimately, the idea of you as a separate, lacking, damaged self collapses. Your logical mind can no longer buy into this false idea, and you're released into the boundless space of consciousness that is luminous, alive, and eternally present.

## Out of Your Comfort Zone

This path of freedom invites you to venture outside your comfort zone. When you're living as if conditioned patterns are real, you may not be happy and fulfilled—but you're in familiar territory. So even though you wish for things to be different, you tend to keep playing out the same patterns in how you spend your time, the choices you make, your way of relating to others, and how you think about yourself.

Why do you cling to the ways you suffer? As humans, we have fear-based brains wired for survival, so we feel safest when we're living in the known. We feel safer with a mind filled with familiar self-critical thoughts, and we are fearful of one that is spacious and open. We get used to feeling diminished compared to others, and we're afraid of what will happen if we're self-assured and empowered.

And you may feel that you don't deserve to be happy and content. It's the nature of the identity of believing you're unworthy to ask, "Who do you think you are to be happy?"

This is why what's offered here is so radical. It invites you to get comfortable with discomfort, to *not* know how to think, feel, or react. If the way things are now isn't working for you, then you'll need to step out into a way of being that is fresh and new.

Without the identity of inner brokenness to mislead you, you'll stop seeking approval and worrying about being liked. You won't tell yourself that you expect to fail or that you don't matter. The whole dynamic in your relationships may change, and you'll look at the possibilities for your life in a whole new way. Finally you're out of your comfort zone and in the universe full of potential. You're innocent, like a baby, not knowing, curious, and eager to explore.

It's exciting, hopeful—and scary. As these false ways of thinking about yourself lose their grip on you, how do you relate to others if you aren't needy and broken? How do you feel in your body without the pain of feeling alone and unworthy? What happens to your mind space if you're not busy criticizing yourself?

I was working with Suzanne, who was often overcome by sadness, disappointment, and fear. I suggested that she imagine putting these emotions in the back seat of the car so she could take the steering wheel and be the one in charge. With wide-eyed wonder, she said, "I have no idea how to be without these feelings driving me." Whatever she said, felt, thought, or did from this new perspective was guaranteed to feel different and uncomfortable.

When the identities you hold dear truly begin to fall away, you will feel strange, with no road map that tells you how to feel, be, and act. So here's my advice: Get comfortable with discomfort. Be okay with—and even excited about—not knowing. Because you're now connected with the space where something fresh and new can emerge.

See how every moment contains the seed of possibility? Our suffering becomes a signal to determine what's false and what's true, and we realize the immensity of life's intelligence that is right here, always available to show us the way through to truth.

Notice the fear and negative thinking that divert you from the peace you really want. And respond with a fierce commitment to uncover the core of your true nature, right in this moment that is already whole and fulfilled.

## Open to Life

It's thrilling to shed an old pattern and let yourself not know how to be. Finally, you stop trusting your negative and limiting thoughts, and instead rest right in the space of not knowing. What happens now without the familiar thought patterns? Instead of needing to fix, analyze, and ruminate, which are all functions of the mind, you're now open to respond to what life is *actually* bringing you.

No longer distracted by a busy mind, you notice naturally arising inclinations that you've unknowingly overlooked—perhaps a desire to be in nature, situations that are asking for your attention, a shift in priorities, or the need for rest and self-care. When I invited Josie, a talkative client, to slow down and reflect, she was immediately aware of the conditioned tendency to fill up space with words and how this tendency was draining her family members. Once she was quieter, her true desire appeared, which was to listen more. When you realize how dissatisfying it is to live in the pressures of the thinking mind, you're available to clarity, insight, and peaceful living.

The sacred return to the immediacy of this now moment is an end to being caught in contracted beliefs that make you suffer, and it's the beginning of flowing in harmony with life. To support that shift, I encourage you to experiment—and I'll be offering suggestions along the way to help you. This is the fun part! You get to play as if you're whole and free—because you are. You get to imagine and test out what you would do or say from the space of infinite potential. You get to mess up and flounder and pick yourself up and try again. And you experience how the world responds when you show up as you truly are—your full, unique, beautiful self, peeking out from behind the veil of unworthiness.

Your thoughts underlie your unhappy, desperate reality. And when you're not driven by your thoughts, you're free and unfiltered. You're open hearted toward others because your attention isn't stuck in your mind constantly thinking about your own situation. Simply said, you're open to life.

Here is your first journaling exercise. At the top of a blank page or on a blank screen, write, "What do I really want?" Let that question come alive in you, then spend at least five minutes writing out whatever arises. In this exercise, you're starting to connect with the deepest part of you, which is already free.

## Summary

This chapter introduced the four guiding principles and the five core practices that are the foundation of the approach to finding your way through the self-belief that you're inadequate and lacking. The principles provide clarity about programmed identities and the path to releasing them. The practices guide you to discovering the peace available at the heart of any moment. Together, they point you to the sacred return to your true nature, where you experience everything as fresh and alive.

The next step on our journey is to deeply understand identity. If this open and loving field of awareness is always here, how do you come to believe that you're unworthy? How does the vastness of who you are constrict into limiting beliefs? We'll examine these questions and how they relate to the first two guiding principles in the next chapter.

# CHAPTER 2

# EXPLORING IDENTITY

The only growth there is, is the freeing of the sense of separation.

—Lester Levenson

I was speaking with Melissa, who was denying her own feelings and railing against her current life situation. She hated the medical symptoms she was experiencing and was frustrated with her daughter's lack of communication. She was holding on tightly to wanting things the way she wanted them, even though these were things she couldn't control.

Her resistance was so strong that I had to tread carefully. As we gently explored her reactions, finally she softened. She relaxed just enough to become aware of what she was actually experiencing in the moment, and worlds opened up. She felt the deep fatigue in her body from always taking care of others and discovered how much she was needy, emotional, and longing for rest and care. Identifying as the caretaker and all that entailed was the source of her problems. Now that that was on the table, we could begin to untangle the distorted beliefs and meet the underlying emotions.

This chapter is about bringing to light the nature of identity. How do we come to think of ourselves as the one required to be in charge of others' needs or the one who must keep accomplishing goals in order to feel worthy? The more you understand what these identities are and how you get caught in them, the more you can recognize them when they appear. You need to know when and how you're stuck so you can find your way to freedom.

## Describing Identity: Two Guiding Principles

An identity is a constellation of thoughts and feelings that are so highly conditioned that you believe they define you. You live in the world expecting to be rejected, and you constantly feel anxious. You compare yourself to others and feel hopeless because you come up lacking. You feel like you have to mold yourself into what others want in order to escape the empty hole inside and get their love and approval.

The first guiding principle describes conditioned identities. It says:

> The identity of "I am not enough" (or "I am inadequate" or "I am unlovable") is made up of distorted thoughts that view the self, others, and the world through a lens that is limited and false.

When this distorted view of things is in charge, it's as if a film has descended over you so you're not seeing things clearly. Rather, you're looking through a murky lens of feelings and beliefs and interpreting everything through this lens. If this identification is unexplored, it can seem absolutely real to you. Left unexamined, it's a driving force that can create a lifetime of suffering.

When you're captured in an identity, where is the peace of your true nature? You're focusing on thoughts, trying to figure everything out while your unexplored emotions swirl like a dust storm, and you can't imagine it being any other way.

But there is another way, which is what the second guiding principle tells you:

No matter how real it seems, the identity of unworthiness is optional. You don't *have to* be defined by it.

Reawakening to the possibility of peace in the midst of this onslaught of programmed thoughts and feelings requires you to deeply understand the nature of the personal identity and how it affects you, because the only true solution to the suffering it brings is to realize that your personal identity does not represent the truth of who you are.

Barbara is an acquaintance whose limited beliefs about herself define her. Her self-worth is built on her children's accomplishments and good behavior. She pushes them to succeed and feels worthless and unloved when they act up. The effects of this mind-set are widespread. She tries to please her children, hesitates to set appropriate limits when they misbehave, and overdoses them on after-school activities. She is constantly on edge and far from being peaceful and relaxed.

Can you see how living according to these self-beliefs limits her options and leaves her no space for new ways to respond? If she wasn't attached to viewing her children's behavior as a way to feel secure within herself, she would naturally take them as they are, nurturing their individual preferences and allowing their vulnerabilities and missteps without taking them personally. She would be available to enjoy her role as a mother.

The story you tell yourself about how you're not good enough cannot be fixed by shifting to a better story. There are myriad self-help books out there that will try to teach you to love yourself more or to learn to believe that you are enough. They'll have you looking in the mirror and telling yourself that you're okay or saying affirmations that just don't ring true. This perspective contains a fundamental misunderstanding. It presumes that the identity of lack is real and that the solution is to fix it, or to change it into some other, better identity.

But this identity itself is essentially false, and attempting to fix it will never give you the enduring peace you truly long for. It's like trying to fill up a bucket with a hole in the bottom. You keep putting water in, but it keeps emptying out because you're not getting to the source of the problem.

If you're trying to develop a better identity, you'll end up living in the mind-set of "if only." If only I tried harder to change… If only I believed those affirmations… You think that happiness will arrive at some time in the future—if only all the conditions are in place to make it possible.

But happiness—or peace or loving presence—isn't a state that you attain at some future time. It's here always—in fact, right now—as the true nature of reality. As the first guiding principle states, the personal identity is limited and false. And the solution is not to fix it or hope that it changes in the future, but to realize that it's false and discover what's true. The truth of who we are beyond the personal identity can be discovered in any moment, which tells us, as the second guiding principle states, that the suffering this identity creates is optional.

What a relief to know this! You can give up the trying and effort it takes to figure out how to become fulfilled. Once you've lost interest in the painful thoughts and feelings that make you feel unfulfilled, you realize that the essence of who you are has always been fulfilled. It's not a matter of finding something you don't have, but of discovering that this truth, your essential wholeness, is already the case.

I never cease to be amazed by this possibility. We can buy into our conditioning and delude ourselves into believing a false and divided view of reality. Yet in any moment, with some knowledge about our conditioned patterns and a simple shift of attention, we can be free of the effects of the patterns and experience what is absolutely real—the nondual, undivided space of our true nature as loving, aware presence.

Emma came in for her session humbled by the power of this understanding. She told me that in the past week she had diligently studied the situations in which she felt irritated. She became aware of the stories she was telling herself about these situations, and the personal beliefs that held the stories together. She navigated through these conditioned patterns each time they appeared until they no longer grabbed her.

Clearly seeing into her thoughts and deeply welcoming her emotions, she then had the insight that this freedom from her personal stories was possible in virtually any moment, no matter what the situation. She couldn't contain her excitement about the possibility for her whole life experience to be affected in such a profound way—always infused with truth.

Believing the personal identities that make you think you're separate from life is at the root of your emotional struggles. Our goal in this chapter is to understand how these identities are created and maintained so you'll be able to spot them. And once you bring awareness to them, they start to lose their power. In any moment, you're free to experience the sacred return home to your true nature.

## How the Past Affects You

At the core, you're naturally innocent, and the truth of you has never been touched by any experiences you've had. See if you can get a taste of this right now. Subtract all the events of your upbringing, how you were treated in your early relationships, everything you've learned from others about who you are, and the views you've developed about yourself, the world, and others. That's a lot to subtract! And what remains? Here you are, still here, breathing, open, aware, and alive, not knowing how to be or what to do next.

Now add back in the events of your early years, your relationships with your parents or caregivers, and the messages you received about life and yourself, and that aliveness quickly becomes masked.

Those experiences and ideas stick like glue and seem to so clearly define you. How does that happen?

When you were an infant with an undeveloped brain, the world was a changing array of perceptions that came through your senses. You experienced sight, sound, taste, smell, and touch. And you were oriented toward others, inclined to bond with those around you.

Your body is biologically primed for survival, and as an infant you were entirely dependent on others to get your most basic survival needs met. For example, when you were hungry, which is immediately perceived as a threat to your physical survival, you screamed for attention, terrified that this need wouldn't be met. Your body was in an extreme state of stress until food appeared. Then, getting the nourishment needed for your survival, you were soothed back into a state of relaxation and contentment.

When these basic needs are reliably met, infants develop a sense of security and trust. They learn that crying signals their caregivers to respond to them. As others validate and fulfill their needs, they start to trust life, feeling secure in the sense that they won't be left lacking.

But suppose that Mom is overwhelmed with her responsibilities, depressed, or too strung out to respond. For some reason her heart is closed; she is so stuck in her own story that she can't be attuned to the needs of her child. The infant is left engulfed in strong and uncontrollable feelings, panicking about his very survival. If this scenario is repeated often enough, the infant will stay in this sustained terror or will split off from this feeling and go passive and numb. Either way, the feelings he experiences take up residence in the body. With no capacity at this young age to make sense of the situation, the body lives in a perpetual state of fear and contraction, shielding itself against the world. The natural state of relaxation is lost, along with the ability to return there.

Fast forward to a few years later when the thinking mind is more intact, and this young boy will begin to wonder what is wrong with

him that makes adults not attend to his needs. He'll begin to identify as broken, damaged, and unworthy of love. He has no tools to
address the despair he feels. Living under the spell of this belief,
everything about his being communicates this unworthiness. He
walks with his shoulders rounded and his head held low. He relates
in the world as if he expects to be rejected—and not surprisingly,
the world complies. Or maybe he has the eyes of a hungry ghost,
always scanning outside himself to try to get his needs met.

## The Role of Emotions

Emotions play a guiding role in the development of conditioned
identities. You naturally experience emotions in response to things
that happen in life, and when your emotions are recognized, you feel
seen, heard, and acknowledged. If your caregivers were attuned to
you and your emotional experience when you were young, you
learned a powerful lesson: that you're okay even if you're experiencing emotions. You develop skills to meet them and the confidence to
know that emotions won't last forever and don't have to define you.

But if you were rejected, denied, or criticized for experiencing
emotions, as many of us were, you're left figuring out what to do with
them. Michael learned to repress his upset when he was admonished
for crying. Tracy went into her room and obsessively organized her
clothes when her mother wouldn't speak to her for days.

If there's no loving space for our feelings, they go underground
outside of conscious awareness, and they feed the identity that we're
separate from life. We live on the surface, figuring out how to function, while we cut off and deny this most important aspect of our
experience. We feel fragmented and alienated from ourselves,
making choices we don't understand. It makes sense that our attention would get focused on our thoughts, trying to come to grips with
this confusing reality.

And while we believe what our thoughts tell us and let the feelings sit there unexamined, the quiet stillness at the heart of every moment is ignored. Our attention is captivated by the personal drama we live in, and the peace of our true nature has no space to be felt, let alone expressed.

Offering a welcoming invitation to emotions changes everything. You take the position of awakened awareness and let the fragments of pain come out of the shadows. This is how emotions are liberated from their tendency to solidify your personal, diminishing identities.

Chapter 6 is devoted to emotions—what they are, the value of accepting them, and how to meet them. For now, when you think about your own story:

- What conclusions did you draw about life from the experiences you had when you were young?

- Did you learn that you could trust others, or were you left feeling insecure?

- How are you playing out these messages about trust and lack of trust in the world?

- Can you see that this way of being in the world was learned—that there was a time prior to all of these events when you existed without it?

Life is full of disappointments, including the tiny ones that bury themselves in our bodies and minds. If we don't have the capacity to understand them clearly and take care of our feelings so they don't stick, sad and limiting self-beliefs set in. These beliefs live within us unquestioned until a crack in the conditioned identity opens. Out of desperation and the knowing that there must be something more, we put out a prayer to know our essential wholeness. We reason, quite accurately, that there must be something more than this unsatisfying and anxious life we live.

As part of the animal world, we're built to experience ourselves as separate entities because of our need to survive. And as humans, we create stories in our minds that become the blueprint for our reality. But who we are is not the entity living this story and feeling these emotions. The story draws our attention to our thoughts and masks the limitless nature of our true reality. When we wake up from the dream of the story, we experience ourselves as we truly are—unmasked, untethered to any beliefs, and fully alive. We realize the end of suffering, moment by moment.

## Deeply Understanding the Separate Identity

You can support this revealing of your true nature by deeply understanding what conditioned identities feel like. How do you recognize when limiting thoughts about yourself have undermined your happiness? Get to know intimately what you're experiencing in any moment. If you're peaceful and free, there's no problem. If any of the qualities I describe below are present, then you're caught in painful ideas about yourself that are waiting to be unwound. These qualities describe subtle—and not so subtle—ways that you suffer.

### Compulsive Thinking

When you're caught in conditioning and you don't realize it, the mind gets going trying to figure things out. Compulsively repeating stories, deliberating about "should I or shouldn't I," remaining stuck in thoughts of confusion, worry, and neediness—this mental activity is a sign that tells you you're holding on to conditioned beliefs about yourself that haven't yet been explored.

Conditioned thinking will always tell you that something's not right. For example, suppose that you think you need attention from others in order to feel whole. Right away, alarm bells sound. The brain senses that something is missing and needs to be found, the nervous system gets charged up for fight or flight, and the thinking mind scrambles to understand what's happening and figure out what to do: *How can I get his attention? I can't stand it when he ignores me. What can I do to make him notice me?* The mind spins endlessly.

If you're not aware of this process unfolding, your attention stays locked in thought. And this nonstop, repetitive, fear-based thinking, although it is what you are most used to and aware of, will never solve the problem.

While you're compulsively thinking, what is being ignored? Expanding your attention beyond thought, you realize that the expansiveness of your present-moment experience also encompasses the breath, physical sensations, sense perceptions—and the space of being aware that these arise in. Settling your attention into present-moment awareness, the thought pattern about not being whole loses its power, and the need to think begins to fade. You notice that this being-aware space itself feels surprisingly whole.

## All About "I"

When your attention is gripped by a conditioned identity, most of your thinking refers to a personal "I."

- Am I safe?

- That makes me sad.

- I'm scared.

- I'm not good enough.

- Will he like me?

- I'm offended by what she said.

Everything you think refers to me, me, and me. In your mind, you're living this story with you as the star and your name in neon lights.

But the story is distorted because it's not seeing reality as it actually is. The veil you're looking through is all about your personal wants and needs—what you don't have and what you need to be happy. It interprets the reactions of others according to the belief that you don't matter or that you need to be the center of attention. You're prone to feel hurt and disappointed.

The solution to this suffering is to bring your attention right into the experience of this personal "I" to explore it. Notice thoughts of lack and neediness, the sense of self-importance and being right. Are these thoughts you? What emotions are also present? You might notice sensations of burning or contraction in your body.

When these experiences are allowed to be fully present, you're clearly seeing the identity of personal inadequacy. As you come to realize that it isn't telling you the truth, the "I" story begins to dissolve. A very different—and delightful—way of being appears when the sense of "I" isn't interfering with the flow of life. Without the personal story in charge that limits your view, you find a sense of ease. You're open and available to life.

## Physical Tension

If you are the star of your own story, your attention is drawn into these self-referring thoughts and the feelings that go with them. And it sticks to these thoughts and feelings like glue. Always looking out for yourself, trying to be safe and fulfilled, you're tense, anxious, and constantly on edge—because your present-moment experience is one of lack.

When your focus is no longer stuck to these personal, negative thoughts, you'll notice you're more expansive and relaxed. What happens to the energy that's now free? You're available to show up fully to life as it appears to you in any given moment. You have space to be empathic, nondefensive, and creative without needing anything back. And you see people and situations clearly rather than through the veil of your own personal needs. The simple word for it? Happiness.

## Searching Outward for Wholeness

If you find yourself constantly looking out in the world for what you think you don't have, you've been captured by an identity that just isn't true. The story paints you as a victim who is missing what you need to be happy and leaves you dependent on others to fulfill those needs. You end up waiting for the actions of other people to complete you, while you feel powerless and empty. Can you see how holding on to this victim story will never get you what you think you need?

The invitation is to give up your efforts to try to fix this broken story and turn your attention from "out there" to "in here." You stop searching for wholeness and look right into the heart of the problem: believing the thought that you're deficient and the emotions that go with that belief. You come to know that the content of this thought is not true, and it doesn't begin to define the magnificence of you.

Looking deeper into who you are beyond this thought reveals the vast space of presence. Your attention expands in this endless space, and you realize that everything you experience is part of it—and that "you" aren't separate from it. Ultimately you realize there's no division between "in here" and "out there." There's only an illusion of a separate "you" who is lacking something—it's not actually real. What is real? You, the being-aware space, which is everywhere, stable, empty, and unmoving. Here, the search for wholeness ends.

## Unconscious and Automatic

When you're playing out the separate identity, you're not consciously awake to what's happening in the moment. It's the nature of conditioning to lull you to sleep in your life, which leaves you merely going through the motions of living. Your body shows up and you play out a role, but you're a machine, not actually aware of the thoughts, feelings, and perceptions happening in your direct experience. In reality, you're constantly making choices, but you don't realize it because you're in a rut, automatically living out conditioned habits.

You keep ending up in relationships with a partner who doesn't treat you well, or you unknowingly sabotage your success over and over. The same pattern of experiences keeps happening—you feel the same feelings, do the same thing, and get the same result. It seems to be a mystery as to how you always end up with the same problem.

But if you slow things down and shine the light of awareness on what's driving you, you wake up to the rich fabric of beliefs, assumptions, feelings, and physical sensations that have been arising and influencing you. Now it becomes possible to not be caught in their grip. As the old pattern starts to dissipate, you see yourself, others, and situations with fresh eyes. New responses arise that help you wisely navigate situations you encounter. You're now alive to the here-and-now experience of this precious life.

Start becoming aware of how your conditioned patterns affect you with this journaling exercise. At the top of a page or on a blank screen, write a few words that describe one idea or belief about yourself that defines you or keeps recurring in your mind. Spend ten minutes writing about how this self-definition limits you.

Can you find:

- Compulsive thinking?

- The story that's all about "I"?

- The physical tension that tells you something is wrong?

> *§* The tendency to search outward in the world for what you think you're missing?
>
> *§* The unconscious and automatic quality that defines conditioned habits?
>
> Repeat this exercise for three more beliefs you hold about yourself.

## Running from Your Experience

My client Jill is a beautiful, capable woman in her forties with a very troubled past, including physical, emotional, and sexual abuse. As a child, she would often escape from her unhappy home into the surrounding wilderness with her closest companion, her dog. Here was the only place she felt any comfort.

Decades later in her life, much of this trauma remains unexplored. As a result, Jill is prone to taking things personally and has a hair trigger temper, ready to lash out at others in anger rather than feeling the hurt and pain she experiences. She sabotages any success in her career, quitting when things get tough. She denies that she's good at anything, even though everyone around her can see her sparkle. And she can't trust enough to sustain a loving relationship. This half-lived life of denial will continue until she is willing to unearth the driving force behind these behaviors and explore the pain and what lies beyond it.

When this insidious identity of not being good enough is in charge, even though you may not realize it, you're resisting your present-moment experience. And as the saying goes, "What you resist persists."

Resisting your experience means that you avoid facing what is actually happening within you. You live in the constructed reality of believing that you're inadequate, which lets this belief dictate your life circumstances. You may even be slightly aware that there are unexplored feelings running the show, but you rationalize why you can't turn to meet them.

Humans are built to seek pleasure and avoid pain, so your automatic response is to resist your experience, especially when it's uncomfortable. After all, who willingly wants to be uncomfortable? Who wants to face the dark shadow of emotions without knowing what they'll find?

You may unconsciously resist turning toward your experience, but in doing so, you're saying no to life. But the truth shining through you beckons you to go inward. You stop the knee-jerk reaction to avoid pain, and with a deep exhale and a heart on fire for peace and clarity, you turn to meet what you've been avoiding. Finally, you say yes to all that is being offered to you.

## *How You Resist*

Living according to your conditioning means you're not open to being aware of all that you're experiencing in the present moment. The limited identity you hold about yourself as unworthy thrives on unconsciousness, and if you resist turning inward, it stays firmly intact.

And what are you resisting? The thoughts, emotions, sense perceptions, and physical sensations that are the core elements of your present-moment experience.

Here are some examples:

-  John is a master at staying busy. He skates on the surface of his life, filling it with projects and adventures so he can avoid the unease that sets in as soon as things slow down.

-  Melanie is afraid she's not measuring up at work. She can't wait for that glass of wine at the end of the day to dull her feelings.

- Anne believes she's not good enough to be accepted as she is. To avoid the pain of this belief, she runs herself ragged looking for ways she can help the people around her.

- Judy is terrified of being bored, so she spends hours on the phone every evening gossiping with friends.

We've come up with an infinite array of ways to avoid just being still and experiencing what's here. If you do anything too much—eat, drink, talk, worry, think, clean, exercise, isolate—you're engaging in a compulsive behavior and you're ignoring the feelings and belief systems that motivate this behavior. You're a hamster running endlessly on a wheel, and you'll never be free unless you stop and turn to look at what you're running from.

But as you explore your inner reactions, please have great compassion for yourself and the challenging experiences you've had in your life. You couldn't control much of what happened. You did the best you could. And, like most of us, you didn't have the guidance that might have helped you find your way through the suffering. No matter how badly you've wanted to find the solution to this identity of worthlessness, you just didn't know what to do. That's exactly why I'm here walking this path with you.

The world, by its very nature, is the expression of division. Just look at the tragedies occurring every day. We discriminate based on gender, race, sexual orientation, and political views. Wars begin because of judgments people hold about what's right and wrong. All of this strife stems from attachment to personal identities and stubborn points of view.

The wish to awaken from the dream of one's conditioning is rare, but that is what got you here today. You are willing to stop hiding from pain so you can see through separation and realize the truth—that every single thing that arises is at its source this one, stable, loving presence. This is the presence that welcomes everything just as it is. You've made the decision to bring the light of consciousness to your experience, and it's the most important decision you could ever make. When you feel shame and regret about what you've come to believe about yourself, remember this. Walking this path transforms not just you, but it brings another sliver of light to the shadow of unconsciousness everywhere.

Get to know how you resist your experience. Complete these sentences with as many responses as come to you.

I believe I am _____.

I believe the world is _____.

I believe people are _____.

Holding on to these beliefs makes me _____.

I avoid what I'm feeling by _____.

The things I do too much are _____.

I avoid being still by _____.

I think too much when _____.

I go numb when _____.

## Summary

The four guiding principles are facts about your experience that orient you to what's true. This chapter introduced the first two guiding principles, which have to do with conditioned identities. First, the identity that you take yourself to be is made up of distorted thoughts that are limited and false. And second, believing this identity—and enduring the suffering it brings—is optional.

We saw how our early experiences created conditioned patterns that we live by. Painful feelings that we couldn't manage were pushed outside of conscious awareness, and we drew conclusions about ourselves and the world from how we were treated.

I identified five qualities of suffering that will help you recognize when you are living through the veil of a conditioned belief about yourself:

- Compulsive thinking

- A personal story that is all about "I"

- Tension signaling that something is wrong

- The tendency to search out in the world for what you think you need

- The unconscious and automatic quality of living a conditioned habit

Finally, we shed light on how and why you resist turning toward your inner thoughts and feelings, and how this resistance sustains the pain of conditioned identities.

The next five chapters cover the five core practices that invite you into the spacious and loving field of your true nature—the sacred return. We'll start with "turning toward your experience." Maybe for the first time, you'll press "pause" on all the ways you resist what's happening so you can say hello to the unexplored beliefs and emotions that have been driving you all along. It's the return home that ultimately brings the peace you long for.

# CHAPTER 3

# CORE PRACTICE #1: TURNING TOWARD YOUR EXPERIENCE

There is a life force within your soul—seek for it.
There is a priceless jewel within your body—seek for it.
If you are searching for the Ultimate,
Do not look outside yourself. Look within.
That's where you'll find it.

—Rumi

On July 20, 1969, nearly every TV in the world was tuned to watch Neil Armstrong take the first step on the moon. Despite numerous simulations and the crew's vast experience as both pilots and astronauts, the mission ended up being way more complex than expected, especially the lunar landing. At one point Armstrong's heart rate measured 160 beats per minute.

But they landed safely, and with all systems in place, the door to the lunar module opened. Armstrong took that first historic step onto the surface of the moon.

I was a young girl at the time and remember vividly watching those men in their spacesuits at the start of their mission walk across the elevated platform, enter the spacecraft, and close the hatch, ready to go. Can you imagine the qualities it took to journey into space, let alone to land and walk on the moon? How do we muster up the courage to go into the great unknown?

Walking a path outside what we know requires commitment, persistence, dedication, and the ability to navigate any circumstances that might arise. It takes a full and powerful "Yes!" even in the presence of fear.

Here, we are embarking on a different kind of journey than the one Armstrong and his crew took decades ago—the journey to discover your essential wholeness—but the qualities that you'll need to bring along on this journey are similar. You won't be traveling to the moon, but you will deeply explore your inner experience, challenge your assumptions about yourself and the world, and experiment with behaviors that are outside your comfort zone.

If you've been holding on to the identity that you're damaged or inadequate for a long time, you're used to inhabiting your life from a perspective that is negatively biased. The inner journey is exactly what's called for so you can expand beyond this conditioned way of living and know that you are unlimited, luminous, and aware—and free of confining ideas about yourself and the world.

## The First Core Practice

This journey of the sacred return back to yourself involves five core practices, and here we introduce core practice #1. It's called "turning toward your experience." You can think of turning toward your experience as an ongoing invitation. It's the voice of wisdom gently and consistently calling your attention away from your grasping mind and inward to make friends with what's happening within any given moment.

This turn toward your own experience may be new for you, because we tend to look outside ourselves to solve our sense of lack and need. How long have you been searching out in the world for that relationship, situation, or material object that will finally get rid of the gnawing pain inside that tells you you're not okay as you are? How long have you been waiting for Prince or Princess Charming to come and save you?

The truth is that no one is coming to sweep you off your feet and solve all your problems. If it seems like someone is doing that, it will be a temporary fix, at best. And nothing you get from the outside world will ultimately give you the fulfillment you're looking for.

You turn toward your experience to discover something revolutionary—that you're not missing anything and there's nothing wrong with you. Through skillful investigation, you shed the sad and limited identities you hold about yourself. As you deeply understand that these self-beliefs completely fail to accurately describe the essence of who you are, they start to soften.

How you approach this journey matters. If Neil Armstrong had been timid and narrow-minded, he never would have set foot in that space capsule. He needed an adventurous spirit to explore the unknown and the intelligence to navigate whatever surprises came his way.

Likewise, when you turn toward your inner experience, you need to bring to the table four essential qualities: openness, curiosity, kindness, and dedication. We're calling these qualities touchstones because they are qualities that anyone can find within and cultivate.

Whenever you get confused or lost in old habits and ways of thinking, you can reorient your attention by finding and grounding yourself in these touchstones. They are the friends you bring along as you turn toward your experience. The touchstones invite you right into presence, which is where you'll find release from the negative patterns that haunt you.

# The Value of a Conscious Breath

Before we get to the touchstones, one essential tool to have in your toolbox as you turn toward your experience is your ability in any moment to take a conscious breath. Just about every client I've ever worked with naturally takes an expansive breath, almost a sigh, when they first realize that their attention has been captured by a conditioned thought pattern. This breath is like a homecoming. It breathes life into the body that's been closed down and forgotten by endless mental activity, and it helps the mind to open beyond a habitual and contracted line of thinking.

Conscious breathing calms the nervous system and acts as a reset for your in-the-moment experience. It takes you off the treadmill of patterns that play out automatically so you can choose with awareness and intention instead.

Try a conscious breath right now. You'll naturally breathe more slowly and deeply than normal. Make the breath three-dimensional as you consciously expand your ribs in the front, sides, and back as you inhale, and let all the breath go as you exhale. Pay attention to the sensations in your body as you breathe. Now try it one more time…slowly and deeply, using the full capacity of your lungs.

Keep conscious breathing as a tool in your back pocket. It puts the brakes on your conditioned patterns and opens you to the experience available right now beyond any separate identity. Now that you're aware and breathing, let's explore the touchstones.

# Openness

Openness is the touchstone that helps to untangle your programming. We all know what it's like to be stuck in familiar patterns that define our everyday reality. In fact, isn't this how most of us live? We experience the same reaction we've had a million times, and we still don't know what to do about it. We draw the same conclusions about our self-worth, and can't find another way. Although we may not realize it, we're reacting automatically—like a programmed robot—closed off from considering new ways of thinking and feeling.

Being open invites you to recognize that these thought patterns are rigid and confining and that they present a false picture of reality. If you plunge forward caught in the tunnel vision that assumes these thoughts are true, you already know the outcome. You'll feel defeated, frustrated, and resigned to suffering.

Observe young children for a window into openness. For many of them, the world is an amazing wonderland. Not yet restricted by conditioned habits and low self-worth, they're infinitely creative in how they think and play. When you're not hampered by old habits that aren't serving you, you too can reclaim this same sense of wonder.

As we explore the identity of lack, see if you can find the child in you who isn't limited and lacking. She's the one who is open, innocent, and awed by life.

## Fresh Possibilities

Being open offers fresh possibilities. You start to question the beliefs you hold to see if they are actually true. You adopt a position of wonder, spontaneity, and not knowing. You stop accepting the drudgery of same old, same old, and you consider that perhaps you've been missing something potentially transformative while you've been lost in the fog of feeling worthless and deficient.

I was in a session with Mandy, who constantly gave unsolicited advice to her adult children. She couldn't keep from offering her views on how they should handle even the most mundane situations in their lives, and her children resented her for it.

As I invited her to be open to her experience, she noticed strong feelings of self-doubt and a gnawing agitation in her midsection. She was surprised to discover how intensely she wanted to control her children, and she didn't like what she saw. As she took time to open fully to the pain of her actions, she began to contemplate new behaviors and ways of being with her feelings. Once she saw things clearly, she was sincerely motivated for her actions to reflect love and not her personal need for control.

## How to Be Open

That's the power of openness. You open to what is here in your experience, and you're courageous to know the truth. Only then can you tap into the natural wisdom that is always here to guide you. You stop defending and avoiding. You stop thinking you have all the answers. You begin to have an inkling that perhaps the limiting ways that you think about yourself may not actually be true.

What are you open to?

- Exploring how your mind makes you believe you're unworthy.

- Understanding the nature of emotions and how they grip you.

- Considering new ways to respond in familiar situations.

- Contemplating who you are. Who is this "I" who hates herself or feels she needs the approval of others to feel whole?

- Resting your attention in being aware, in the sense of pure being, which is here at the heart of every moment.

## The Ease of Not Knowing

When you're open, you move beyond what you know and you enter the land of not knowing. It's a land where you stop expecting things to turn out the way you think they should and where you quiet your assumptions about yourself and others.

Steven is an acquaintance who lives a good part of the time thinking he knows how things will turn out in the future, and these ideas are mostly negative. *I know that store won't be open on Sunday. I'm sure that project won't get finished on time.* These thoughts contain an expectation that he'll need to go without the things he wants and leave him feeling sad and frustrated. They show a fundamental, conditioned mistrust of the world, an assumption that life is stingy and withholding rather than generous and full.

When you think you know what will happen, you're usually assuming the outcome will be unpleasant.

But adopting an "I don't know" perspective means just that—you don't know. You don't know if the store will be open or the project will be finished on time. Then you're open to all possibilities. And admitting that you don't know is aligned with the truth. Can you absolutely know what will happen before it occurs?

And consider this: You don't know if you are unworthy. You don't know if you're damaged. Instead of assuming that you absolutely know these beliefs to be the essence of who you are, the touchstone of openness invites you to take an "I don't know" perspective. It's a very good step when you can honestly say, "I don't know who I am." Can you feel how freeing that is?

I want to be clear that I'm not asking you to believe the opposite—that you are perfect as you are or that your true nature is not lacking anything. If it were that easy, your suffering would have stopped a long time ago. I'm asking you to do something unconventional, which is to put everything you think you know up for grabs and to simply not know.

If you're honest with yourself, what you've known until now hasn't brought you the peace that you're longing for. So here's the option: Be fed up with what you know—the pain of feeling inadequate, the idea that you're worth nothing unless you get approval from others. Let these ironclad belief systems crack open so the light of truth can seep in.

There absolutely is another way than the one you've taken for granted for so long. And it starts with being open.

> Let's experiment to get a taste of openness. First, close your eyes, and take a deep breath. Now, bring the experience of open space to your body. Imagine space permeating your muscles and flowing through your brain. Let space into any tension you're experiencing.
>
> As you breathe space everywhere, your shoulders drop and your belly softens. Let the sense of yourself open into the space beyond the boundary of your body.
>
> Now, bring to mind a situation that feels stuck in your life. With this open brain and body, free of stuck beliefs, brainstorm new ways of responding.

## Curiosity

Curiosity is a close sibling to openness. It's the touchstone you bring with you as you turn toward your experience, inviting you to explore, investigate, and ask questions in any moment that you feel taken over by feelings of worthlessness. Are you wallowing in self-doubt, unable to move forward? Then start getting curious about your in-the-moment experience.

As humans, we are naturally curious from birth. We want to know, understand, and make sense of ourselves and our world. Have you seen an infant captivated by his toes or a toddler asking endless "why" questions? When we're curious, we come from a place of not knowing, and we're open to clarity and understanding.

Many years ago, I was traveling in Nepal. I was in a remote village with some Nepali friends, and we were returning to Kathmandu with an eight-year-old boy who had never before ventured farther than the surrounding villages. We walked about a day and a half to reach a road where we would board the bus to Kathmandu.

I will never forget the look of absolute awe and amazement on this boy's face when he first saw a bus pulling up to the stop. A moving box with people in it! How could that be? And when we arrived at our room in Kathmandu, flicking the light switch totally captivated him, as he made the light appear and disappear.

Where would we be without curiosity? Every building, every scientific development, every system—everything human-made began with someone being curious to understand or to know how something works.

When it comes to finding our way out of our human-made suffering, harnessing our natural curiosity serves us well. If you want to untangle the belief that you're going to be rejected or that you're worthless unless you get approval from others, then bring curiosity to your experience.

Shine the laser light of awareness within, on what's happening right now, to understand how it is that you convince yourself that a happy and fulfilled life is not for you.

Consider my client Charlotte, who told me that she feels like a fraud in her career. When I hear a general statement like that, my curiosity gets going, and I start asking questions. What does "fraud" mean to you? When do you feel like a fraud? What triggers it? What are the thoughts in your mind telling you? What feelings arise? How do you feel in your body? What do you feel like doing or saying? What else is present besides this identity of "fraud"? And these questions are just the beginning.

If you want to be free of the self-beliefs that limit you, be so curious about your in-the-moment experience that you become an expert on how you suffer. Being curious will help you know the elements of these patterns so well that you begin to notice them when they arise. The behaviors that were once automatic come to conscious awareness, and you are primed to make a choice that frees you from suffering rather than reinforces it.

With an attitude of curiosity about her experience, Charlotte became intimately familiar with the inner voice telling her she's a fraud and realized that she can recognize when it's likely to arise and how it makes her feel. When she notices it on the spot, she now has the option of being present where she is without the underlying commentary from this negative self-belief. So freeing! In the chapters that follow, you'll learn how to do just that, but for now feel into the possibility of deepening your curiosity about your in-the-moment experience.

Instead of assuming that you know, take an "I don't know" perspective. What is this breath? How is it that thoughts gain their power to color your whole world? What is a thought, anyway? We don't know the answers to these questions unless we stop and directly look at our own experience.

## How to Be Curious

Curiosity is partly about figuring out how things work. If you want to understand the plumbing under your kitchen sink, you'll take out a flashlight, get down on the floor, and begin tracking where the pipes come from, where they're going, and what their function is. You'll notice a series of insights: *Oh, this is the drain out, this one brings water in, this one is the hot water and this one the cold water…*

Likewise, when you get curious about your own experience, if you're like me, worlds open up. You might notice:

- When I feel awkward, my body is tense and contracted.

- When I'm anxious, there are thoughts running in my mind nonstop.

- The longing for love comes with heaviness in my chest.

❀ When I feel lonely, my body is very agitated.

Being conscious of what happens in your experience is a starting point to bringing an end to patterns that aren't serving you.

And as we explore further, you'll discover something beyond the ruminating thoughts and painful feelings. You'll see that there is a field of presence in which these thoughts and feelings arise. And when you bring your attention here, you're peaceful and relaxed.

## Ask the Right Questions

For many of us, especially those who have been around the block when it comes to psychotherapy and self-help, we're prone to asking why. A feeling arises, and you wonder why the feeling is present—that is, what circumstances in your life have brought about that feeling. You ask: "Why can't I find my life's passion?" "Why am I still afraid?" "Why didn't my parents love me?"

The problem with asking why is that it draws your attention into your mind to answer the question with more stories about what happened. It takes you away from being present now. But if you take the "why" question to its essence, you'll see that what you actually want is happiness and peace. What you are really asking is: How can I find an end to this pain? What do I need to do to be happy?

Sometimes it helps to understand the particulars of a given situation. It can help to flesh out the story so you can make sense of what happened. But the path to true happiness is to know our experience directly. Answers to the "why" questions might temporarily satisfy the mind, but questions like these get right to the heart of the problem and help to untangle limiting identities:

❀ What am I actually experiencing right now?

❀ Can I be with these physical sensations without being distracted from them?

- ❦ Can I make space for these emotions to be as they are?

- ❦ Can I let go of struggling right now and see things as they are?

- ❦ Are these thoughts actually true?

- ❦ Is there anything else that wants to be seen?

This way of being curious about what is here is so delicious. You get to know the truth about what you're actually experiencing! It is elegant, simple, and intelligent. And when you turn your attention to what is happening in your inner world, your whole relationship to it changes. What was previously hidden and denied is now seen clearly. You identify the source of your problems from the ground up, rather than trying to figure them out and solve them in your mind.

The touchstone of curiosity invites your attention into the present. Being curious offers the potential to see things in a new way and brings fresh eyes to stale views of yourself and the world. Why not start asking questions right now?

Turning your attention toward your inner experience, be curious. Bring a sense of wonder to your questioning. Focus more on the questions without being so concerned about the answers.

- ❧ What is present right now?

- ❧ Letting go of labels and just experiencing it, what is it? How does it feel?

Don't answer these questions in your thoughts. Instead, just be with what you experience and notice what you feel. If you think anything, try, *Oh, it's this,* or *Oh, it's like this.*

# Kindness

When you turn toward your experience with curiosity to explore the identity that tells you you're worthless and inadequate, you might find it difficult to accept what you discover. You might find the needy one or the one who you wish could have handled things differently. The touchstone of kindness softens the edges.

Everyone has the capacity to be kind and compassionate. Kindness toward yourself and others is your natural state in the moments when you realize you're not the separate and limited self defined by your conditioning. When fear, judgment, and the need for self-protection fall away, what remains is love, and any action that arises is powered by love. Kindness is one of the expressions of love.

Rather than judging yourself, regretting what happened, or living in wanting what you don't have, you find that you're open to all that arises with a kind and loving heart. Kindness is the medicine for feelings that might seem impossible to bear or the shameful memories that swirl around and keep you from being present. It's the touchstone of mercy, acceptance, patience, and love.

## How to Be Kind to Yourself

You don't need to wait for kindness to naturally appear. In fact, you can be kind and welcoming to your own experience starting right now. Whatever is arising in you in this moment, start by saying "Hello." And I mean this literally. Say "Hello, shame. Hello, unworthiness." I know it may sound silly, but be a friendly host and welcome these experiences rather than slamming the door in their face and turning away. Whatever you experience is here, so why not make friends with it?

What does it mean to be kind toward yourself? I was sitting with Jeannette, who couldn't grasp the idea. Then her eyes lit up. "Oh, you want me to treat myself the way I treat my dog!" Whether the model for you is how you treat a dog, a child, or your best friend, you apply that deep acceptance toward yourself and your own experience.

When you're kind, you're walking with yourself. You don't abandon the tender energies that come up in you or betray yourself by turning away from whatever appears. You let feelings be present without judging them or pushing them away. When you notice a harsh and critical voice in your mind, you take a conscious breath and accept the hurting part of you that has somehow come to believe that you're not okay. When a familiar pattern arises over and over, instead of dismissing it with "Oh, that again," you welcome in the one who is suffering, as if for the first time.

And the "you" that I'm speaking to is the unbounded capacity for acceptance. It's the unconditioned you, the relaxed space that has no agenda and receives everything as is. It's the truth of you that is naturally capable of love. You *can* rediscover this truth within.

## Deep Acceptance

Kindness toward yourself may not be your strongest quality, but it's one to cultivate with diligence. Because the solution for the identity of lack and unworthiness won't be found by looking outward into your relationships or life circumstances. No matter how much you long for it, it's just not possible to get enough positive attention to plug up the hole that makes you think you're beyond repair. And if this has been your identity for a long time, you know it won't disappear on its own, so you need another approach.

And here our approach is to look right into the hole, to bring to light the shame and deficiency and to meet those feelings with the love, attention, and care you've always wanted. This is why kindness toward yourself is so important. *You* are the most reliable source of this deep acceptance. You *are* the wholeness that you're searching for.

Kindness includes paying attention to what you need—and what you want. It's okay to count yourself in, give yourself a break, and treat yourself with supreme generosity. In fact, it's perfectly natural to do just that.

> Can you turn toward your inner experience right now and befriend what's here with the deepest acceptance and kindness? If you were to be infinitely kind to yourself, what three things would you do?

## Dedication

When you're dedicated, you want something so much that you devote your whole heart to it. You're enthusiastic and committed. You let yourself be fully invested, and you persevere even when things are challenging. Can you feel the power of dedication?

In my work helping people find their way to peace and happiness, changes don't happen immediately, but we patiently carry on. Over time, my clients understand how thought patterns take hold, and they learn to feel into the wave of emotions in the body. Then, one day, I'll know that the cloud of negativity is starting to lighten. Mark found the confidence to end a relationship that wasn't serving his happiness. Victoria, who was shy and introverted, joined an organization and was asked to be on the board. And Rachel became curious about her emotional needs when she realized how they were affecting her family. These turning points happen with dedication to the process of shedding distorted identities.

Long-standing conditioned patterns have a powerful momentum behind them, which is why dedication is essential. They start with a thought, such as *Something is wrong with me*, which is reinforced over and over until it becomes a belief. By the time you've reached the end of your rope with this emotional pain and are willing to contemplate a new way of being, it seems like you have a formidable task ahead. Enter dedication.

## How to Be Dedicated

Every moment of intelligent inquiry into your experience matters. Like a sculptor creating breathtaking beauty from a stone with each tap of the chisel, repeatedly turning toward your experience chips away at conditioning to reveal you in your natural innocence, unencumbered by limiting stories.

In the end, it doesn't matter if these programmed reactions keep appearing. As humans, we're feeling and thinking beings who react to the world around us, and we're physiologically primed to survive, protect, and keep ourselves safe. This means you *will* react and you *will* experience emotions.

But with dedicated practice and the fire for truth, you'll learn to meet these human reactions with an exquisite sense of attunement to your in-the-moment experience. You perceive an old story or emotion starting to take shape, and you see it for what it is—a temporary appearance that arises in the space of being aware. And if an emotion starts to stick, you meet it with friendliness, feeling its power but not letting it drive you. This is fully conscious living, welcoming the flow of experiences but not being caught in their spell. In time, you'll discover the ultimate release, which is the freedom of realizing that these stories and emotions don't define who you are. You're no longer attached to them.

Kathy arrived for her appointment absolutely elated. She told me that she had been diligently welcoming feelings of ingrained, persistent anxiety, which was a whole new way of relating to these feelings. She was thrilled that she had barely felt anxious in weeks. She reported: "Before, I thought I had to combat it. I tried to breathe it away or exercise it away."

And now? "I accept it. I notice the bodily sensations that I experience and feel compassion toward them." So simple.

Be sincerely dedicated to your deepest longing to be peaceful and free.

Complete these statements:

The way the conditioned identity of feeling inadequate and worthless affects me is _____.

The fire for freedom feels like _____.

If I were sincerely dedicated to finding peace, I would ____.

## Summary

This chapter introduced the first core practice, which is to turn toward your experience. Whenever you recognize that you're sad or needy, know that you don't have to let that feeling continue to consume you. You can turn your attention toward what's happening within, which begins your exploration.

As you turn toward your experience, carry with you the four touchstones—openness, curiosity, kindness, and dedication. Instead of assuming that things will continue to be the same, be open and take an "I don't know" perspective. Then get curious about what is making you suffer. Welcome whatever you find with great love and compassion, and rinse and repeat. Each time is the sacred return to the truth of who you are.

In the next chapter, our journey deepens as we explore the second core practice: the safe haven of being aware. Once you turn toward whatever you're experiencing, you'll learn to relate to it with intelligence and compassion.

# CHAPTER 4

# CORE PRACTICE #2: THE SAFE HAVEN OF BEING AWARE

Do not ask me where I'm going.
As I travel through this boundless world,
Every step I take is my home.

—Dōgen

Valerie interprets just about everything her husband says through a veil that tells her that she's at fault. He doesn't say anything about the meal she prepared? She concludes that it wasn't tasty enough. He doesn't comment on how well she accomplished some banking tasks? She thinks he's judging her.

Valerie grew up with an alcoholic father who rarely gave her positive, loving attention. She tried desperately to please him, but nothing she did could ease his pain or calm the chaos in her family. Her husband's silence reactivated this old belief that she will always fall short, along with the remnant of the sad little girl who so wanted to please others and make everything right.

I suggested that, in the moments when she feels dismissed by her husband, she acknowledge the presence of this little girl in her and welcome the thoughts and feelings that appear with great kindness. Rather than the familiar route of going into the story of what is happening, she could simply accept the experiences as they arise. Then I invited her to expand her attention beyond these objects into the surrounding space of present-moment awareness and to rest there. She was silent for a moment, taking in this possibility, then stated with conviction, "I could easily do that."

Even I was surprised at the power of this one simple invitation to explore possibilities outside the limited identity of believing she was wrong, bad, and not good enough.

You may not be able to make a shift like this so easily at this point, but keep applying the concepts you're learning here, and you will start to feel better moment by moment. Valerie's example shows a window into what's possible for you, too. She's living the second core practice—finding freedom from the sense of personal lack by opening to the safe haven of being aware.

## What Is the Experience of Being Aware?

We know what it's like to be aware of something. If I ask you to look at the tree outside your window, you turn to look and become aware of the tree. If I ask you to notice how you're feeling in your body, you'll become aware of some physical sensations. But there's something else going on in these moments that you may have never noticed before. There is the object you're aware of (the tree or the physical sensation) *and* the experience of being aware.

This "being aware" experience is not an object like a tree. It's the background experience prior to witnessing any object, and it's the fundamental ground from which everything arises. You can think of it like the space in a room that has to exist for you to perceive the objects in the room. Or, as teacher Rupert Spira (2016b) explains, it's like the screen on which a movie plays. When you're watching a movie, you're absorbed in the story and unaware of the screen. Yet the visual images of the movie couldn't exist without the background on which they are projected.

I know that finding this being-aware experience can be challenging. Quite naturally, we look for it in our minds or try to find it in the environment. But it's closer than that—it's the pure sense of being present. So we'll go slowly so you can get a taste of it.

When you're struggling with interpretations of situations that leave you feeling inadequate and you're propelled to seek attention from others, your focus is on objects—other people and your own thoughts, needs, and emotions. These objects seem to be your reality. But in those moments, as in every moment, there is also the background experience of being aware, the realm in which these objects appear.

How can this awareness help you? When you withdraw your attention from the objects that make you suffer and shift attention to the experience of being aware, two significant things happen.

First, your in-the-moment experience immediately changes. Where before you were completely caught up in the story of yourself and your personal inadequacies, now you're in a place of stillness and presence observing these thoughts, feelings, and reactions. We commonly call this mindfulness, but knowing the safe haven of being aware goes beyond observing objects. You begin to notice that as this observing presence, you're not emotionally reactive. You're simply here, observing.

You might be noticing strong emotions or a thought storm of how unlovable you are, but you as the presence that notices them are calm and stable. From this calm and stable place you can say to yourself, *Oh, here is a feeling of anxiety, here are thoughts judging how I look right now.* Reactions happen, but this being-aware space itself is neutral, welcoming, and at ease.

Second, when you shift your attention to being aware, you begin to question what's real. As you notice familiar thoughts and emotions, you realize that you don't need to be caught up in them. You're just observing them float through awareness, seeing that they come and go. When you witness your experience rather than being consumed in it, the identity you've held about yourself as broken and needy begins to lose its power. How could this identity really be "you" if you feel so much more relaxed and open with the simple shift of attention to being aware? Are you *actually* broken and needy?

Perhaps these beliefs and the feelings that come with them appear and disappear in awareness and don't have to define you. Perhaps, when you don't feed them with your attention and simply observe them instead, they begin to feel less real.

This powerful questioning gives you a small taste of the possibility of being alive and free, maybe in a way you've never felt before. Behind the veneer of personal needs and limitations that you thought were so real is the simple experience of being aware. By noticing it, you're developing a new relationship with your thoughts and feelings.

Consider my client Bill, who is easily annoyed when he comes home from work and finds that his sons have left the house a mess—again. His mind gets going with thoughts of blame, frustration, and failing as a parent. I invited Bill to move his attention out of these stories and to be aware of what he was experiencing in the moment. With some gentle prompting, he accessed the tender place inside him that felt anxious and agitated when he saw the mess. He remembered this feeling from early in his life, when he was left to fend for himself as a young boy in a house that was always in disarray. He became the observing presence for these feelings, allowing them to be present.

In the moment when he is aware of these feelings—rather than being caught in their story—he can offer them the compassion and acceptance they need. This process of discovery showed Bill that there was so much going on that he hadn't been aware of—memories from his past, feelings of frustration, the physical arousal in his body, and a desire to control his sons' behavior. He learned to lovingly open to the fullness of his in-the-moment experience. He gradually became more understanding of his sons and much kinder toward himself.

As you'll come to see, the space of being aware is a safe haven. It's always there for you at the heart of any moment, and by its nature it is free of troubling thoughts and feelings. It doesn't judge or avoid anything—it welcomes everything unconditionally.

When I work with people who are very engaged with the challenges of their life story, I often guide them to take a time out, close their eyes, and disengage with the thinking mind. Even if it's just for a moment or two, they usually experience a palpable stillness and sense of peace. This is what's possible for you in any moment. You can stop, breathe, and be.

## Guiding Principle #3

The guiding principles that help you find freedom from identifying as inadequate or undeserving point you to the truth of your experience. The first two guiding principles describe how negative thoughts about yourself are distorted and how believing them is optional. The third and fourth guiding principles, which focus on what's happening right now, will help you discover the spaciousness of being aware.

Guiding principle #3 is this:

You have control over shifting your attention to different parts of your experience.

If I ask you to pay attention to your next inhale, you'll stop reading—that is, you'll stop focusing on and making meaning of the words on the page or screen, and you'll become consciously aware of the sensations that come with taking your next inhale.

And if I ask you to explore the sensations you feel in your body, you'll scan your body and notice a fluttery feeling in your belly or tightness around your neck. Other things are happening, but you are consciously placing your attention on a specific object.

Even though it may not feel like it, you always have control over where you place your attention, and this choice is monumental. It means you can be consumed by fear and panic, or you can open to being aware of your in-the-moment experience. You can be diminished by what your thoughts tell you, or you can tap into the freshness of what any moment offers you. You can suffer or be peaceful.

You might find it hard to control what you pay attention to because for so long your attention has been glued to certain objects. If you always think of yourself as limited and incapable, your attention is glued to thoughts that tell you that story. If everywhere you look you experience disappointment and rejection, your attention is glued to that point of view.

The invitation of the third guiding principle is to take back control over the precious resource of your attention by untangling your attention from the objects that bring unhappiness to your life. This is something we actually can do. Usually we try to do the impossible—which is to control things that are uncontrollable. We want to control other people's behavior so they do what we want them to do, we try to control situations so they come out in our favor, and we want to try to control our thoughts so they're more positive and not so intrusive.

But, with enough awareness, we *can* control what we pay attention to.

Notice that instead of thinking, you can pay attention to sensations in your body, look at what's around you, or open up to hearing sounds that maybe you haven't noticed before. Try willfully moving your attention around right now.

I know that challenging thoughts will continue to grab your attention. But just for now, notice that it's possible to have a little control over where your attention goes. Be patient with yourself as you get used to having this choice.

When I first began to play with this idea of having control over my attention, I was amazed at what I discovered. I observed that I was living a reality I created by feeding fear and inadequacy. My mind was constantly scanning any situation I was in to see if I was safe, running a constant track of questions: *Am I okay? What does she really mean? Did I do the right thing? Did I miss something? Should I have done something differently?* It was endless! And my attention was so glued to those thoughts that I didn't realize how much tension was present in my body.

No wonder I didn't feel at ease. How could I possibly be light and happy with that ruminating tape playing nonstop below the radar of awareness? The discovery that I didn't have to pay attention to that tape was a revelation. In the moments when I witnessed those thoughts rather than believing what they were telling me, I felt a great sense of relief. The thoughts could be present, but I didn't need to make them real. I didn't need to define myself by them. Without being caught in their story, I realized I could breathe, see, listen, sense, open up, wonder, or just be. And when I did anything other than reinforce the story, I felt so much more alive.

Now it's your turn to try it. Without doing or changing anything, commit to taking a few hours to notice where your attention goes. Maybe set an alarm on your phone to go off every half hour, and when it rings, simply notice where your attention is. Are you thinking? What thoughts are you thinking? What stories are you telling yourself? What patterns of thinking do you notice? What emotions are you experiencing?

If you're like me, you may be very surprised by what you find.

# Guiding Principle #4

Guiding principle #4 tells us that:

> There is more to your experience in any moment than your thoughts and feelings.

During the times when these limited thoughts about who you think you are have taken hold, it seems impossible to see yourself in any other way. These thoughts seem to completely define your reality.

But now you know that it's possible to shift your attention away from these thoughts—even if it's just for a few seconds. Not being engaged in the story they're telling you, you become aware of so much right here in the moment that you've been missing. You hear the sounds of people talking in another room, you feel the breeze on your skin, you see things like chairs, trees, and books, and you feel the sensations of your breath as you inhale and exhale. This array of phenomena has been here all along—you just didn't notice it. And opening your attention to notice what else is here in addition to thoughts is a pathway out of the negative thinking mind.

There's even more here than the things you see, hear, think, and feel, and that is the experience of being aware. Let your attention fall away from these objects just for a second and you'll notice that something remains—an energized sense of aliveness. You won't find this aliveness by thinking. It's just here as the undeniable fact of your present-moment experience.

This timeless presence that is always here at the heart of every moment is pure. It's not filled with thoughts telling you you're damaged and unlovable. Focusing your attention on this presence, and not on the contents of your mind and emotions, you realize that there's a part of you that isn't damaged. This part is perfectly okay and accepting of what is. And you notice that when your attention rests here, you're peaceful. You may not consciously know this right now, but this peacefulness is who you *actually* are. That's right. You are not the one described by your self-criticisms and self-doubts. You are this aliveness that is already whole and free.

You may be so attached to the contents of your mind that you can't find this being-aware experience. But you may be more familiar with it than you realize. Have you ever been caught up in the flow of doing something enjoyable, not realizing that time is passing? Laughed uncontrollably? Experienced a burst of happiness or joy, or a heart opening that bubbles up from nowhere? Felt an uncanny sense of connection with everything? These are moments when the thinking mind is at rest, and you're fully experiencing the reality of the moment without any mental interference. You're present and alive.

When we have experiences of being one with the moment, we sometimes say that we lose ourselves in them. But this is when we actually find ourselves as we truly are. When we're not thinking about what's wrong with ourselves, we find the unending peace of our true nature.

We don't have to wait for these special moments to occur. This being-aware experience, and the ease that comes with it, is always here. When you're lost in the drama of feeling unworthy, awareness hasn't gone anywhere, it's just been overlooked. Relax your attention away from doing, fixing, changing, searching, and believing your sad story, and you'll discover the safe haven of being aware. Even if it's just for a moment, you've gotten a taste of peace.

This is a three-part exercise. First, take a few conscious breaths with your attention on the sensations in your body as you inhale and exhale.

Now let go of focusing on the breath, and open up to all of your experience. Notice that objects (thoughts, feelings, and sensations) are arising, changing, and passing away.

> Make a simple shift to bring your attention to the field of being aware that these objects are arising in. As this awareness, realize that you're awake, alive, and peaceful. You notice the objects, but they don't affect you. Be like the sky, vast and open, as clouds of thoughts and feelings move through.

## Beyond Survival of the Human Body

If our true nature is awakened awareness and not the personal identity as a separate, limited, inadequate being, then why don't we easily know it? Why do we suffer when suffering is optional?

Part of the answer lies in the brain and nervous system of the human body. As physical entities that are part of the animal world, we're built for survival. This means that we are programmed to be constantly aware of the environment we're in so we're prepared to react quickly to protect ourselves. As Charles Darwin (1859) discovered, the fittest among us survive, so those mechanisms for vigilance and protection are highly developed in us.

Picture a panicked gazelle in the African savanna being chased by a hungry lion. The brain of the gazelle is wired to perceive even the slightest movement that indicates a threat to its existence, and when that threat is perceived, the nervous system kicks into flight mode to preserve the gazelle's life at all costs.

Most of us aren't being chased by hungry lions, but our brains contain primitive structures, together called the limbic system, that still function as if we are. Lying deep in the center of the brain, these structures are designed to first recognize danger, then trigger other parts of the brain and the nervous system to react to the danger. In milliseconds virtually every cell of the body is primed to fight, flee, or freeze. The limbic system reacts primarily and instinctively with the most basic emotion, fear.

As humans, we also have well-developed higher brain structures, called the cerebral cortex, located in the outer layers of the brain. These structures allow us to think, reflect, solve problems, use language, and add meaning to our experience. If we're not aware of these thinking processes, they lean toward the negative, a tendency known as the negativity bias. After all, they're here to protect us from danger, so they're oriented to bring our attention to what's wrong or not okay. Sound familiar?

We're built to run on fear and to view the world as a potential threat. We're so caught in the mind-set of separation that wants to keep us safe that we forget that being relaxed is even possible. No wonder we suffer! And no wonder the still, peaceful experience of being aware can be so hard to find.

But there are cracks in the armor of these protective inborn bodily processes. Our nervous systems enjoy the state of relaxation, our brains are capable of pleasure, and we have naturally released hormones that incline us toward love and connection. Picture a mother gazing with wonder into the eyes of her newborn baby. The brain is firing to create this lovely experience as well.

But there's something beyond the brain and body, something beyond our conditioned identities about who we are and even beyond the human experience of pleasure and connection. Before all objects and any thoughts about them is the boundless space of awareness that encompasses everything. Since awareness naturally accepts everything as it is, nothing is seen as a threat, and nothing needs to be protected. The mind-based personal self fears risk and needs to play it safe. But from the point of view of awareness, there's nothing to fear. Awareness just is, fully alive and completely accepting.

When your heart is racing and your mind is telling you you're about to fail, you may not realize it, but the experience of being aware is here. When you're thinking that you're unlovable, you're also aware. When you're feeling lonely, empty, or lost, yes, you're still aware. Your attention may be subsumed in these thoughts and feelings, but the simple possibility always exists to disengage from the contents of the mind-created stories you're living and rest in the space of being aware.

Then the human life looks very different. You're untethered from your ideas about yourself that keep you from fully experiencing life, and you realize the compelling freshness of everything, finally free of judgments and interpretations.

This aliveness is always your safe haven. Whenever you're caught in the suffering of the mind, you're playing out your human destiny that is built on fear, lack, and discomfort. But whenever you notice that these tendencies have taken hold, you can return to the safety of awareness that holds everything in the arms of love.

Reflect on a time recently when you felt afraid or threatened. Recognize that:

- The limbic system in your brain perceived danger.

- Your nervous system automatically started firing to prepare you to fight or flee.

- The thinking processes were interpreting the situation to help you protect yourself.

Now, shift your attention to the safe haven of being aware. Just for a moment, let go of engaging with the threat, anxiety, and pressured thoughts. Have compassion for the fearful one who tries so hard to be safe. Recognize that you can notice these reactions while you're also peaceful and aware. Be this noticing presence.

# Getting Familiar with Being Aware

The first core practice asks you to turn your attention away from the world and in toward your own experience, and the second core practice invites you to recognize the fact of being aware. Resting in this spaciousness, you have a new relationship with challenging thoughts and feelings—and this new relationship is powerful. You begin to contemplate the possibility that these thoughts and feelings misrepresent the truth of who you are.

Why is this being-aware space your safe haven? Why can you trust it?

**The experience of being aware is always here, always accessible.** Thoughts come and go and even mountains that seem so solid are constantly changing shape; situations change, and people come in and out of your life. But the reality of being aware is absolutely reliable. You can trust it completely because it is unchanging, ever present, and never not here. You can always, in any moment, rediscover the welcoming presence of being aware.

**Being aware is by nature peaceful.** Just as the ocean has no problem with any of the sea life that appears in it, awareness, the background of all experience, is completely at ease with whatever objects arise. Can you imagine the ocean saying it doesn't like a particular fish or wave? Resting in being aware is just like that. The mind may judge, reject, and agitate. It may tell you nasty things about yourself, creating drama and difficult feelings. However, if you rest as awareness, stories may arise, but that doesn't mean you have to involve yourself with their content. Feelings appear, but they don't have to disturb this peace.

**Being aware is being fully alive.** When your reality consists of mind-created ideas that limit and divide, you can't possibly feel fully alive. Your attention is busy with the depleting task of trying to make sense of your needs and disappointments. When you rest your attention in just being aware, you're no longer involved with the contents of your mind. This is revolutionary! Now that you're not feeding worry and confusion, you come alive to the ordinary experience of everyday life. No longer resisting anything, you actually live with enthusiasm, appreciation, and often joy.

**The experience of being aware is naturally intelligent.** Resting attention in awareness clears the confusion that comes from the beliefs of your personal, limited, inadequate self. The personal self runs on fear and seeks protection at all costs. Losing this veil of threat leaves you undefended and open to the natural intelligence of life. With your attention on the being-aware experience and not on objects, you're able to see through the psychological workings of yourself and others, so it becomes apparent how to respond from love and not from the fear and need of the personal sense of self. By listening deeply instead of reacting in a familiar pattern, you might find that you're free to speak authentically with people or to exit situations that are toxic or damaging. You set limits, take appropriate action, and generally respond in ways that are inherently loving and life-affirming. You're one with the unfolding of life, flowing like water.

## The Magic Is in the Moment

I corresponded by email for months with Jane, who begged me for help with her troubled marriage. At first, she couldn't stop blaming her husband. Whenever she looked within, the turmoil she found was so overwhelming that all she could do was resort to complaints once again.

But I kept supporting her longing for peace with quiet invitations. One day I received an email and I knew her mind-set was starting to crack open. She told me that she untangled her attention from her angry mind for some moments and was able to experience expansion and relief. She began to find the peace of her true nature—one moment at a time.

And this is how it is for you, too: *the magic is in the moment*. You don't need to be concerned with changing who you are or figuring out a new way to be that erases your painful past. It's impossible to solve all your future problems. What we're doing here is much simpler than that, and it boils down to the moment.

The only time you're suffering is now, and the only time you can let go of the turmoil of personal stories is also now. Your experience in this now moment may be a culmination of what happened in the past. But the only thing that's real is what's here right now. And if you want to be free of the weight of feeling that something is wrong with you, that freedom is only available now.

Right now, in this moment, there is an endless space of awareness that is completely at ease with things as they are. In the next moment, the mind may rev up again and grab you, but looking with clarity about how things are *right now*, you're not broken and there's nothing wrong. You—as your true nature—are whole, luminous, and infinitely peaceful. And this is what's true in any moment.

Until the shift toward the safe haven of being aware begins to stabilize, it's completely normal to find yourself caught over and over in these painful identities that don't serve your happiness. And, if you're like me when the idea of the personal self started falling away, you'll get caught hundreds of times a day.

Remember the touchstone of dedication? There is a great power in knowing what you want and dedicating yourself to that. Keep in mind the peace and freedom that are absolutely possible, and keep doing what's necessary for you to know these experiences intimately.

Always remember that the magic is in the moment—this moment. Realizing that your attention has reglued itself again to thoughts and feelings is a moment to celebrate. You're now aware of what's happening! Here is your opportunity to stop and recognize the story that your thoughts are telling you about your personal value.

- Instead of feeding this story by thinking it and assuming it's real, move your attention to your breathing.

- Instead of embellishing the drama of your emotions about how someone hurt you, open your attention to the physical sensations appearing in your body.

- Instead of focusing on any objects such as thoughts or physical sensations, rest your attention in pure aware presence and experience the peace of your true nature.

And do the same for the next moment…and the next…and the next. This is how your problems and habits change. There's nothing to analyze, nothing to solve or figure out. And it takes no time at all. Realize that you're suffering, right now, because your attention has grabbed on to personal thoughts and feelings. Then, right now, disengage your attention and let it rest here, unattached to any personal concept.

Your mind will tell you that finding freedom in the moment isn't enough. It will say that you should always be peaceful and that these mental habits shouldn't recur. It will admonish you for not practicing enough or not doing it right. The mind is running on the assumption that if you were truly free of these painful identities then they would never again visit you. But none of this is true.

Conditioned programming recurs—that's its nature. It pulls you into ruminating about the past and worrying about what might come. But enter the timeless now and you're home. It's eternally here, the all-encompassing, naturally accepting field of presence that holds everything with love.

# Summary

The second core practice is the safe haven of being aware. Applying the guiding principles to the times when you feel lacking or inadequate, you realize that these self-identifying thoughts are limited and distorted descriptions of who you are (guiding principle #1) and that believing them is optional (guiding principle #2). Knowing you have control over where your attention goes (guiding principle #3), you open to the space of awareness that is beyond your thoughts and feelings (guiding principle #4).

We explored the qualities of being aware. This field of awareness is always here. It's receptive and peaceful. And it's intelligent and fully alive. Understanding the inborn functions of the brain and body tells us that, as humans, we're conditioned for survival and not for resting peacefully in the moment. The space of being aware is a place beyond the body and mind where we still embrace our humanness.

"The magic is in the moment" means that we don't have to be concerned about always trying to be aware. The only time we can be aware is in this timeless moment, and we can return here over and over. Resting in awareness is the safe haven from the pull of suffering.

Now, in chapter 5, we get to thoroughly explore the mind. How do thoughts work to derail our happiness? How is it possible to find freedom from the mind? I hope chapter 5 is a mind-blowing experience for you.

# CORE PRACTICE #3: LOSING INTEREST IN THOUGHTS

All your problems are just thoughts.
And thoughts are not a problem.

—Jeff Foster

"I can't stand all these thoughts. They're driving me crazy. Can you please tell me how to get rid of them?"

I can't tell you how many times I've been presented with this question. And I have great compassion for the one asking it. If worrisome, shameful, and distressing thoughts occupy your mind, then of course you are desperate for relief from them. You just want them to stop bothering you and interfering with the peace of mind you'd love to experience.

Unfortunately, no one can give you the magic fairy dust that will make your thoughts stop, change, or disappear. And that's why this chapter is so important.

You may be able to quiet your mind for periods of time, but this is not a sustainable solution to the thinking that tells you you're never going to be good enough. And if you take the advice to change your negative thoughts into positive ones, you're going to get even more entangled in thinking. While you're telling yourself that you're perfectly okay as you are, at the same time you're not believing it. And this digs you deeper into conflict—and suffering. You might even feel *more* inadequate because you can't successfully change your thoughts. This is an inner war that doesn't serve your happiness.

So what do you do with those depressing thoughts of lack and inadequacy that you know don't serve your happiness?

Thankfully, there is a solution—the third core practice, called "losing interest in thoughts." In this chapter, we'll look so deeply into the nature of thoughts and thinking that paying attention to these highly conditioned thoughts just won't make sense anymore.

This chapter dives deeply into the first and second guiding principles:

- Believing thoughts about yourself leaves you looking through a lens that is limited and false; and

- Defining yourself by these thoughts is optional.

You'll learn to recognize thoughts and see the wisdom in not letting them rule your world. And you'll discover how to use thinking as a tool to support being free of the limiting identity that you're unworthy.

## Thoughts 101

We're so caught up in the stories our thoughts tell us that we don't stop to question them. So let's start by considering what a thought actually is.

Before you read any further, take a moment to bring your attention inside and see what you notice when you ask that question. Close your eyes, and gently float the question *What is a thought?*

You'll notice that a form, usually made up of words, seems to solidify in your mind. This object appears, then at some point disappears. No thought lasts forever. But let's break it down even further.

When you learn a language, you come to associate specific sounds with meaning, and you call these sounds "words." For example, you learn that the sound/word "cat" means a small furry animal that meows. We all agree that certain sounds have certain meanings, and we learn to put these words together to become sentences that we understand. And when these sentences appear in your mind, we call them "thoughts."

A thought signifies something to you only because you've learned what this pattern of sounds means. If a thought appeared to you in a language you didn't understand, it would have no meaning and no impact on you. But when you know what the sounds mean, they have the potential to affect you.

Many thoughts are barely noticed. They come and go, and they cause no disturbance whatsoever. You realize you're cold, and you fetch a sweater. You're in the grocery store and pick up the same container of yogurt you always get. These thoughts aren't problematic because they don't attach to any personal identity. They're fleeting and leave no residue that causes suffering.

But, as you know well, some thoughts can cause trouble. You go to fetch your sweater, and you can't find it. The damaging self-talk sets in. *I always lose everything. I'm so stupid. I should have checked my locker at the gym before I left. I'll never do anything right. Now I'll look ridiculous because I'll have to wear a sweater that doesn't match. And I'll have to go back to the gym—one more thing on my to-do list.* And on and on...

They are thoughts, the ones that attach like Velcro. They're the thoughts that grab your attention, stay in your mind, and color your view of yourself and everything else. They separate you from happiness.

We know in our own experience that thoughts don't have to stick. We think random thoughts all the time that don't affect us at all. So what makes a thought stick? What turns a random thought into the limiting identity that you're inadequate?

Sticky thoughts all have something in common—they refer to you, the personal "I" that you take yourself to be. These are thoughts fueled by agitation or some other emotion. They're highly conditioned, which means they draw your attention in like a magnet. And you believe what they tell you without question.

Recently I wrote a blog post inviting people to write in and disclose the false and limiting thoughts about themselves that they have come to believe.

Vanessa responded: "All my life I've believed that I will never be enough—good enough, pretty enough, smart enough. Now I'd like to rid myself of this thinking pattern. Lately I seem to be attracting people who reinforce my negative thoughts."

Jeannine wrote: "I believe I am flawed and destined to struggle. I got the message that I was not capable of achieving anything I wanted. I am tired and feel it's too late for me."

These conditioned thoughts, which are actually just sounds with arbitrary meanings attached, gain so much power to define us. Can that power be diminished? Absolutely. How? By withdrawing your attention from all thoughts, especially the troubling ones. That's what core practice #3 is all about, and you'll learn the wisdom of this practice in the pages that follow. I know that it may sound next to impossible to lose interest in your thoughts, so I invite you to please stay open to this possibility as we unpack thoughts and the nature of thinking.

## Kinds of Thoughts

First, it's important to be able to recognize the different ways that thoughts appear so you can be aware of them. It will be helpful for you to take the time to do the exercises included for each category of thoughts below so you understand them in your own experience and how they affect you.

## Memories

A memory in and of itself is benign. "My third-grade teacher was Mrs. Barton." "I grew up in a house on Green Street." But when it's about you and accompanied by an emotional charge, it has the potential to stick. So be on the alert for memories that grab your attention and won't let go.

Think of some recurring memories. Start playing with hearing them as a series of sounds that play in your head instead of statements of absolute truth that mean something important about you.

Now write down some of these memories as brief sentences. Look at the words and see the letters as shapes. In this moment, there's just you looking at shapes with no meaning attached.

## Judgments and Opinions

Judgments and opinions divide the world into right and wrong, acceptable and unacceptable. And they seem to creep in under the radar of consciousness and catch you in their grip. Before you even realize it, you're finding fault with yourself or criticizing someone else. Or you're going on about how what's happening shouldn't be happening. Judgments are built on a solid sense of the personal "I," as in "I know what's right and wrong," and "I know how this should be."

Think about how you judge yourself and others. How do these judgments affect you and the way you show up in the world? Can you see how they're negative and divisive? In reality, these judgments are just a collection of familiar sounds. Give these sounds meaning, and you'll suffer. Let them be, and they start to lose their power to define you.

Journal for a page or two on these questions: How do the judgments I hold about myself and others affect me? How do my opinions support or interfere with happiness?

## Expectations

Expectations are a close cousin to judgments. In reality, at any moment anything can happen. When you truly understand this, you're open to the infinite range of potential outcomes. But when you expect a specific outcome to occur, immediately you've narrowed the boundless field to one possibility only.

How many times have you been disappointed because others haven't met your expectations? And if your expectation is that you deserve to be treated poorly or that you'll always fail, life will probably comply.

Come up with three expectations you commonly layer onto reality about what you wish, hope, or think will happen. These sentences might start with "I expect that…" or "I know that…" Write in your journal about these questions:

- How do these expectations resist what is?

- How does this resistance show up in your thoughts?

- What is the effect on your body?

## Doubts

When doubts are in control, you are bound to feel anxious and ill at ease. You spin around wondering if you did the right thing, going back and forth in your mind. *Should I have done that? I'm not sure I handled that well. What should I do?*

Persistent doubts eat away at you when you can't let them go. They're based on an underlying belief that you can't trust yourself and the flow of life.

Next time you catch yourself going back and forth in doubt, ignore the thoughts for a moment and be quiet. You might immediately notice fear or contracted places in your body. And maybe you'll notice the quiet, confident voice of knowing that gets drowned out by the doubt. Notice that you don't *have to* feed the doubt.

## Interpretations: Adding Meaning

There are several ways that we add meaning to situations through our thoughts. We label our feelings or describe what is happening, then add interpretations that become the stories we live by. It might be a fact that your father left the family when you were young. But if you take it personally as a message about your self-worth, this story will impact your quality of life and the choices you make.

It's a normal function of the human mind to seek understanding, but when we leave our conclusions unexamined and take them as true, we're living a reality distorted by the content of these thoughts.

Think of your life story as a movie script. Write down the main story lines. Then, for the person in the starring role—you—reflect on how the meaning you've given these stories affects how you view yourself, others, and various situations in your life. Consider that the stories, and the meanings you've given them, are all thoughts. If your stories stop defining you, what remains?

## "I" Thoughts

Although we take them for granted, any thoughts that refer to a personal "I" potentially bring suffering. *I want… I need… I think…* And who is this "I" the thought refers to? It's the limited, false identity that you think you are. When you believe these "I" thoughts, they pull your attention into your mind and distract you from opening to the whole of your present-moment experience. You can't see situations clearly or be fully available in your interactions with others.

"I" thoughts are inherently stressful and divisive. They're based on fear, and they sustain the idea of an "I" in here that is separate from the rest of the world out there.

"I" thoughts are so common that we don't realize how much they color our reality. Take a day to become aware of any thoughts that contain the word "I." Set your alarm to ring every hour, and when it goes off, reflect back to notice the "I" thoughts. Here are some examples: *I need to get that done. It just started to rain—I wish it were sunny. It's too noisy for me. I don't think she approves of me.* If you're like me, you'll find this kind of commentary running almost nonstop.

Notice that you are pulled this way and that when you pay attention to just about any thoughts, and that peace eludes you. Notice how these different kinds of thoughts separate, fragment, and leave you in a state of not having and being enough. If you believe the content of these thoughts and play them out without taking an honest look at them, of course they will color your view of things.

Gary writes, "I always feel like a victim. Deep down, I'm powerless and unworthy. I try to fill the void with Facebook, eating, and keeping busy."

Gary isn't a victim of circumstances; he's a victim of believing his thoughts. So here's the truth about thoughts—they are sounds with meaning attached. Are these sounds you? They may have become stuck to you and your idea of yourself, but are they really you?

Now I'd like you to be superhonest about how these thoughts impact you. Make a list of the thoughts that bring you pain and suffering. Take your time with this, and be as thorough as you can. Look for memories, judgments, opinions, expectations, doubts, labels, stories, wants, and needs. Your clue will be any thought that somehow refers to you as a personal "I." Now, let yourself feel how these thoughts affect you. What are the consequences for you, other people, and how you handle situations?

Play with viewing these thoughts as a series of sounds without any meaning. They're mental noise. To help with this, pretend the sounds are appearing in a language you can't understand. Are these sounds you—or are they objects that come and go in the space of being aware?

## Untangling from Thoughts

Hopefully, you'll understand by now, at least to some degree, that thoughts that tell you you're unworthy or broken may *seem* to define who you are, but they are not *actually* who you are.

Even with the seeds of this understanding sprouting in you, you may find yourself entangled in your story, judging, criticizing, and expecting the world to deny you approval and love. This is normal, because the attachment to thoughts takes time to unwind.

Christine is learning to spot the thought pattern that tells her she is undeserving and not good enough. During our meetings and with my guidance, she is beginning to trust the experience of spaciousness outside her thoughts.

Yet, just as all of us do, Christine gets overrun by familiar conditioned reactions. She feels compelled to seek attention by being the life of the party and takes it personally when someone else is assigned a project she thinks should be hers. She understands that when she feels these reactions, she's believing thoughts that aren't true, but the power of her conditioning is still strong enough to derail her sometimes.

Penny asked herself in one of our sessions, "What false thoughts am I buying into?" At one level, she knows the thoughts are false, but she still gets pulled to make them her reality.

Be patient with yourself as you become more and more deeply aware that your thoughts don't define you. Sometimes you'll be able to easily turn away from the content of your thoughts, and sometimes conditioned thought patterns will seduce you into believing them. The attachment to thoughts unwinds gradually as you notice them, see them clearly, and commit to finding your way from suffering to peace.

## A Friendly Relationship with Thoughts

When people start realizing the extent to which stressful thinking has overtaken their lives, they just want the thoughts to disappear. Humans naturally seek pleasure and avoid pain, so this response makes sense—get rid of the problematic thoughts and all will be well.

As you probably know, however, this approach doesn't work. If you could easily eliminate thoughts, then that's what you would do, and you would be living happily ever after. But *trying* to eliminate them leaves you fighting with your experience and waiting for peace to come at some future time.

So if you can't stop or change these pesky thoughts that bring you down, what do you do? You start to form a friendly relationship with them.

The first core practice invites you to turn toward your experience with curiosity and openness. Instead of swirling in the content of the thoughts, you open up to seeing them with wisdom and clarity. Invoking the second core practice, you relax your attention away from involvement with thoughts and into the safe haven of being aware. Then, using the third core practice, the thoughts may be here, but you lose interest in what they're telling you.

What could be friendlier? You're not pushing thoughts away or wishing they were different. You're not resisting them or pretending they're not present. You're not waiting for a better time when the thoughts about how inadequate you are won't haunt you anymore.

You do something much simpler. You recognize that they've appeared, and you let them be here without engaging with them. See how you have way more control than you might realize? You can't choose which thoughts float into your awareness—and you can't choose to get rid of them—but you can choose what you do with these thoughts. You can hear them, believe them, and let them rule you. Or you can shift your attention away from them and know they don't have to affect you.

Losing interest in the content of your thinking might sound like a challenging task. We'll get to some ways to help you below, but let's first acknowledge how damaging these thoughts can be.

The inner language of the identity of being inadequate and broken can be so incredibly harsh. There's name-calling, swearing, degrading put-downs, and more. I don't even want to give this extreme language any emphasis by offering examples here, but you know what I'm talking about. You would never dream of talking to anyone else the way you talk to yourself. It's a kind of violence directed inward.

It's a lot easier to lose interest in thoughts when they're not so charged with emotion and negativity. One way to reduce the charge is to tone down the language. Take a careful look at the inner language of the thoughts that appear in you, and see if you can neutralize it. Change it into words that are gentler and more benign. In the spirit of love, peace, and harmony, neutralizing thoughts serves to stop the inner name-calling and severe self-berating.

You might also find that your attention gets stuck cycling around in the stories you tell yourself, and it doesn't want to let go. I have found in my work with people that sometimes stories need to be told out loud to help loosen their grip.

I spoke with Donna, who desperately wanted to be free of the idea of the separate self and the pain it brought her. She couldn't have been more dedicated to exposing herself to the teachings that she hoped would set her free. But still she struggled.

Our conversations revealed hidden stories that were keeping her entrenched in suffering. She was petrified of losing control, and we discovered that being in control and using her mind to solve problems were residual conditioned strategies that had helped her adapt during a difficult childhood. These stories from long ago, and the pain that still lived with her, needed to be lovingly exposed in the light of day.

If you find yourself gripped by stories that won't let go, maybe further investigation into the stories is needed to reveal the subtle beliefs about yourself—beliefs that you don't deserve happiness, or that you'll fall apart if you surrender control. And maybe that investigation needs the support of a therapist or spiritual teacher. Going into the story may be a helpful step along the way, as we meet as true friends in the shared vision of discovering the truth of who you are beyond all stories.

## Ways to Lose Interest in the Content of Thoughts

Losing interest in the content of thoughts is a choice you can make once you're fed up with the pain expressed by these thoughts and you're willing to come home to yourself. It's a fierce choice, because it goes against the grain of profound conditioning and everything you know to be true, and it's a wise one—to turn away from believing what is not actually true. It's a choice that can happen only in the moment.

Withdrawing your attention from the content of thoughts happens right when you realize you're caught in a story. This means you may be making this choice hundreds of times a day in the beginning. And each "No thank you" to the story takes you out of the past and future and aligns your attention with the endless space of being here now. You leave the contraction of a judgment or denigrating label behind as you open to the limitless potential in this now moment. It's so fresh here!

How do you make that loving choice to return to yourself? How do you lose interest in what these thoughts mean to you? When you realize your attention has been gripped by thinking, it helps to start with a full and conscious breath. A breath offers a simple reset of your experience and calms the nervous system. Then try these suggestions:

- ❧ Turn away from the content of thoughts—in your mind and by actually turning your head, symbolically blocking them by putting up your hand, walking away, and leaving the troubling thoughts behind. It helps to include physical movement.

- ❧ Just say no to the story. No thank you, not going there, not interested.

- ❧ Remind yourself how painful they are. They just don't serve happiness; they're not useful.

- ❧ Remember they're just sounds in your head. Hear them as "blah, blah, blah," or as words in a language you can't understand.

In a moment of insight, Kathy exclaimed, "Oh, I can tune them out like my kids tune out my nagging!"

As you play with losing interest in the content of painful thoughts, you might notice the mind arguing with you. It says, *You can't just let that thought go. It's real, I need that one!* This is more thinking—another thought that pulls your attention away from presence. From the safe haven of here-and-now aliveness, sense the pain and misunderstanding of the one who fears the unknown without these familiar patterns of thinking.

This distorted identity—of the you who is unworthy and undeserving—was never who you are. Losing interest in these thoughts, you're spacious and open. Attention seems to expand as the limited thinking mind loses its power. Here, there's breath, life, and the unlimited capacity for receiving what is as it is. You're easeful and loving—free of the personal story, welcoming everything and resisting nothing. These are not just words for you to read. This is the real possibility available right now, your true nature waiting for you to come home.

## Inquiring Into Thoughts—Asking Questions

The direct path to happiness and peace is to turn away from troublesome thoughts every time they appear. Eventually, you're simply uninterested in them. You love the precious reality of being awake to the moment so much that when thought forms appear, you remain open and undisturbed. You love that you can live in wholeness rather than inadequacy!

But sometimes thoughts grab you and won't let you go. In those times of suffering, asking questions helps to loosen their grip.

Say you're embroiled in the mind-set of scolding yourself for something that happened, with thoughts filled with self-criticism and wishful thinking about what you should have done differently.

Take a breath to relax your attention away from believing these thoughts, then turn toward them with openness and curiosity. Ask questions without knowing what answers will come:

- What is this thought? How did it appear? What is it exactly? (Remember that a thought is made up of sounds that you've learned have a certain meaning.)

- Do I need this thought? Is it essential?

- Does it serve me or anyone else? Is it helpful or useful?

🌀 Is the content of this thought agitating, neutral, or relaxing?

🌀 Can I lose interest in the content of this thought?

When you see the thought for what it is—a collection of sounds, meaning that diminishes and separates, content that is not true, and a distraction from peace—why hold on to it? It just doesn't make sense anymore.

Maybe you'll go through this inquiry many times a day when the limiting identity you take to be you is strong and sticky. I have two words for you: Do it! Don't settle for a veiled existence that pretends you're damaged and leaves you hoping for the time when you'll finally be happy. Take control by bringing your attention right into your in-the-moment experience and by investigating to find out what is false and what is true.

---

Bring to mind a single thought that grabs your attention and disturbs you. Go through the inquiry questions above one by one to dismantle its power over you.

Asking questions is a powerful practice that not only exposes the distortions in thoughts that make up the limited personal identity, but a practice that can liberate you from this identity and wake you up to the reality of life as it is right now.

I love asking questions! Instead of knowing or assuming, get out of your mind and into wonder. Try these:

&⸱ What is most alive in me right now?

&⸱ What can I surrender right now that isn't serving me?

&⸱ How does life want to move me?

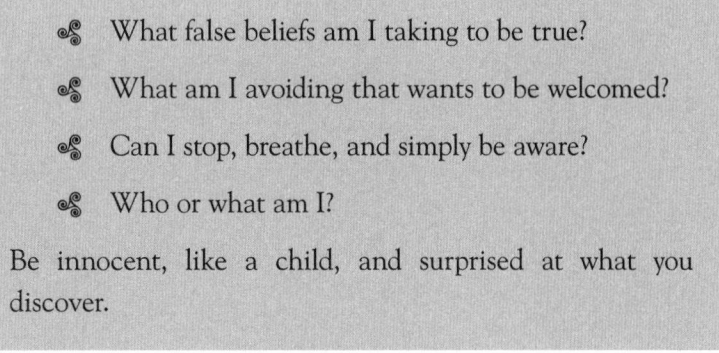

の What false beliefs am I taking to be true?

の What am I avoiding that wants to be welcomed?

の Can I stop, breathe, and simply be aware?

の Who or what am I?

Be innocent, like a child, and surprised at what you discover.

## The End of the Mind-Driven Life

"How will I know how to live without thinking? Won't I sit on the couch like a blob?" These are the words of Mark when he was contemplating life without the limiting ideas about himself that developed from his past. He was so used to relying on his thoughts that he was missing an essential truth: there is an undercurrent of aliveness that is always here, whether or not we're thinking. Can we live without worries or the need to scan for love and safety? Absolutely yes. You don't need the personal sense of "I" to live. And this is what you discover when you take the plunge and go beyond the content of your thoughts. You realize that you function just fine.

From the perspective of the limited self that needs to be vigilant and protective, not relying on thoughts is scary because you're left in the space of the unknown. How can you navigate life without thoughts? Thoughts give you a comforting illusion of control, and to some extent they may be useful: holding on to beliefs about how things are helps you organize your world and know what to expect.

But you're risking your happiness if you get attached to those thoughts. When you believe yourself to be a separate person with a specific limited identity, you tend to focus on the objects of the world, trying to get your needs met. Whereas when you don't invest in the content of those thoughts, they're not driving your choices, and you're simply here, awake and aware. Trying, figuring out, analyzing, worrying, getting, strategizing—these actions fall away as your attention rests in the spaciousness of loving presence. When you're not caught up in thinking, you're open to life as it is. You relate to others with an open heart instead of with fear of abandonment or disapproval. And you take things as they come without resisting them.

I reached a turning point when I finally realized that I didn't need to be attached to any thoughts to live life fully—and that changed everything. The necessary practical thoughts come when they are needed, but the hopes, desires, preferences, and judgments—they are an extra layer over the brilliance of reality and complicate the unfolding of what is inherently natural and at ease.

When we're living the mind-driven life, we end up betraying ourselves. We unconsciously run on conditioned habits that block our essential aliveness, and then wonder why we suffer.

Your opportunity always is to stop, turn toward your experience, find the space of awareness that by its nature accepts everything, and lose interest in the thoughts that appear. When you do that, you'll find that the basis for the painful identity you believe about yourself no longer holds up. Shifting your attention away from what it tells you, you realize you're available to the flow of life. And here you discover a natural intelligence that is way beyond the content of your thoughts.

Try out these experiments to get a taste of the end of the mind-driven life:

    Set aside an hour or half a day when you have no plan for how to spend the time. Sit quietly, and listen. Don't know what's going to happen. Let yourself be surprised by how you're moved.

> ❧ Go to the grocery store with no idea about what you'll purchase. Buy items only when you feel an inner *Yes*.
>
> ❧ Next time you're deciding among different options, stop, let go of thinking, open to the space of aware presence, and listen patiently for what comes.

## Summary

This chapter introduced the third core practice—losing interest in thoughts. We learned that when we look into the nature of a thought, we find that it is a series of sounds to which we've given a particular meaning. This understanding reveals the revolutionary possibility of losing interest in the content of thoughts, in particular the sticky thoughts that make up the limiting ways that we think about ourselves. As the first two guiding principles tell us, believing these distorted views of ourselves is optional.

We looked at ways to lose interest in thinking and introduced the practice of questioning thoughts. These insights reveal that thoughts can't possibly define who we are. The practical thoughts that help us function arise, but there's no attachment and no problem. This chapter also offered a window to the end of the mind-driven life.

To round out our study of the elements of the personal identities that make us feel inadequate and unlovable, in the next chapter, we'll open our investigation into feelings. This is core practice #4: welcoming feelings. What is a feeling? How can it be a doorway to knowing the truth of who you are?

# CHAPTER 6

# CORE PRACTICE #4: WELCOMING FEELINGS

When you are lonely or lost in darkness,
I wish I could show you the magnificent
light of your own being.

—Hafiz

Michelle's living space is loaded with clutter, and her pain related to this clutter is palpable. She longs for peace—both in her mind and in her environment—but she resists any invitation to explore underlying emotions. She knows there is deep sorrow buried within her, but how will she ever experience peace while keeping this feeling at bay?

Feelings or emotions (here we'll use these words interchangeably) are a perfectly natural part of the human experience. Of course you feel! You take in what's going on in your world, and you react to it. You're criticized, and you feel the sting of shame. You experience loss, and you grieve. You react with fear when you perceive danger, whether it's realistic or not.

You can't control the emotions that arise, but you can decide what you do with them once they visit you. You can get more involved with them by talking about them, by trying to figure them out, or by avoiding them—or you can discover a vast, open, and loving space in you that welcomes all your emotions unconditionally. Choosing to welcome them lets all of the parts of you that feel hurt come out of the shadows and into the light of conscious awareness. Finally, they're free to be held with love and acceptance.

This chapter offers you the tools and understanding that will give you the confidence to welcome your emotions. We need this guidance because emotions are a challenging experience for many of us. We just don't know what to do when we're caught in the wave of a strong emotion. We're so scared of experiencing emotional pain that we come up with every way possible to ignore what we're feeling. We suppress it the best we can just so we can keep our heads above water and function. And when the feeling is too intense to be pushed away, it overruns us beyond our control.

When you fight emotions, you're resisting them. You're saying "No!" to this tender part of your inner experience—which leaves you feeling fragmented, confused, and anxious. How do we resist emotions? We disregard them, deny them, ignore them, or pretend they're not here. And we engage in a range of distracting behaviors: staying busy, using substances, shopping, gossiping—anything but actually stopping, noticing our feelings, and letting them be. We want the feelings to go away, but the fact is that they're here. Just as you can't get rid of disturbing thoughts, trying to get rid of feelings just doesn't work.

So what do you do? You stop the inner war with your feelings and come to peace with them. And you can start by invoking the core practices we've covered so far:

- 🪷 Core practice #1: You turn toward your feelings with openness, curiosity, and kindness.

🌀 Core practice #2: You anchor your attention in the safe haven of being aware so you can observe what's here without identifying with it.

🌀 Core practice #3: You lose interest in the story line.

And then you continue with core practice #4: welcoming the direct experience of emotions with love and acceptance.

## What Is an Emotion?

Let's start by getting curious about what exactly an emotion is. What is sadness or frustration or anxiety? When you study your experience of emotions, you'll notice that there are two aspects to them. There is a story running in your mind about the emotion—the label you give it, what happened, a description of how you feel, what you should do about it—and there are physical sensations in your body.

The story focuses your attention on your thoughts so you're involved in a mental commentary *about* your experience—you're not *actually* experiencing what's present here and now. Stories about emotions tend to be filled with dramatic details.

Physical sensations in your body are your in-the-moment experience of emotions. We're usually so captivated by our thoughts, living in our heads almost 24/7, that we don't realize there's a whole world of physical sensations appearing in our bodies.

I recently made a plan with a repairman to come to my home to fix something. He failed to arrive at the agreed-on time and didn't respond to my subsequent messages. My mind seemed to relish the story. In a voice filled with frustration, it kept telling me how unprofessional he was, how he should have handled the situation differently, and how I now needed to spend my time finding someone else to do the repair—all stressful and negative thoughts. And when I opened to what was happening in my body, I felt tension in my neck, shoulders, and jaw.

If you look at any emotional experience, this is what you will discover. If you feel impatient, there will be a story in your mind and contractions in your body. And the same goes with feeling bored, demanding, sad, entitled, broken, angry, or any other feeling.

Check it out for yourself. Take an emotion that you feel right now or have felt recently. What is it exactly? Can you find the story your mind is telling you and physical sensations in your body?

As we saw in the last chapter, you can recognize the story, see that it doesn't serve peace and happiness, and lose interest in the content. You know that you don't *have to* follow this mental narrative—in fact, you're way more at peace if you don't.

But stories steeped in emotion tend to be sticky, making it hard to turn away from them. That's why welcoming physical sensations is so important. If you intentionally bring your attention down to the sensations in the body, you refocus away from the thoughts and invite in this often-ignored physical aspect of your emotional experience. Do this enough, and emotions begin to lose their power to bother you. You realize that sensations can be present without feeding any story. Resting your attention in the space of being aware, you realize that sensations are just objects coming and going and don't mean anything personal about you.

Does heaviness in the chest have to trigger the story about how you were neglected as a child? Do you have to label a fluttery feeling in the belly as anxiety? Is it possible that these are just passing experiences that appear and disappear? Is it possible that you don't have to take them personally?

## How to Welcome Emotions

Our goal is not to get rid of emotions or banish them from our experience. It's to fully let them be here in the moments when they arise. Welcoming emotions in the space of being aware is the healing balm you've been longing for, I promise you. It's the wise way to be that doesn't deny your feelings or dramatize them. Eventually you notice you're triggered less and less. You feel the pull of moving away from yourself and getting involved with the feeling, and you stay grounded in the aware space that deeply accepts the feeling as it is.

## The Art of Welcoming

To welcome something means to meet it with kindness and openheartedness. A friend shows up at your door, and you smile and invite her in for a visit. You create a warm and friendly atmosphere that makes her comfortable enough to let down her guard and stay a while.

Welcoming emotions is just like that. Can you feel into the possibility of meeting your emotions in a warm and friendly way? Fear, sadness, shame, or loneliness arise, and you, as the spaciousness of being aware, open the door and invite them to come in. You offer a loving, safe space that welcomes them.

Here's how. When you realize that you're caught in a swirl of emotions, here is your moment to do something new. Recognize the tendency to avoid your in-the-moment experiences by getting busy in your mind engaging with the stories they trigger. Now stop and take a breath—a deep, conscious breath that anchors your attention and brings some ease to your nervous system. It might help to track the sensations of the breath as you inhale and exhale a few times.

I love this first conscious breath. It's the beginning of shifting your attention away from the story of the feeling and the gateway to returning to presence. The relief you experience with this breath says, "I'm alive and I'm okay. I'm experiencing an emotion, but I'm no longer completely caught in it. I can now take a fresh approach to relate to it."

From the safe haven of being aware, you lose interest in the thoughts that are trying to draw you in, and you notice the physical sensations that are present. Close your eyes so you're present with your experience without being so aware of the outline of your body.

The instruction is simple: from this friendly and open being-aware space, let all the sensations that appear be here. You might notice contractions, vibration, blocks of heaviness, or tiny tensions. There might be tightness, softness, numbness, or space. The sensations may be strong or subtle, dense or light. Take your time with this, and let it be an open exploration.

As you continue to welcome sensations, anything can happen. The sensations might intensify, ease, move, transmute into a different experience, or disappear altogether. There's no goal. Simply stay as the space of being aware and let them be. Have no agenda for them to change or dissolve. Your only job is to be fully with what is as it is, welcoming the way that life is flowing in this moment.

Every time I do this—which may be many times a day—I'm amazed at what I find. Sometimes my whole body is buzzing. Sometimes there's deep stillness with barely any movement. There might be tension in my jaw, or a familiar contraction in my left shoulder.

I don't give these sensations any meaning whatsoever. What do I do? Nothing. I'm just here as presence, letting everything be as it wants to be—for thirty seconds or a half hour or more—until it feels time to move on and do something else. And if a story starts to take shape, I shift my attention back into the body and reanchor as awareness. From here, I lose all sense of any personal self. I experience the sensations so deeply that the awareness and sensations are one, with no separation. I'm completely intimate with what's happening.

This is the safe haven of being aware, the empty space of deep acceptance, which by its nature is effortlessly welcoming. Yes, the emotion may be present, but you know without a doubt that this space is here, too.

This is how emotions lose their impact. You're welcoming the sensations that come with feelings whenever they arise, and with time you discover that the power of feelings to grab you diminishes. There's no longer a need to avoid them or push them away, so they don't build up a residue in your mind and body.

In a moment of pleasant surprise, you might realize you're actually peaceful, where before you would have been triggered. This peace might come as a sense of neutrality and nonreaction, lightness, or well-being. This experience may not last long at first, but you now know what's possible as you stay as the welcoming space for physical sensations.

I met with Rob, who spoke about some very difficult times in his childhood. He told me that later that night he felt a strong burning sensation in his chest that he never had felt before. He didn't try to fix it or make it go away. He let it be present just as sensation, and, surprisingly, he felt grounded and at ease.

Now it's your turn to practice welcoming feelings. Right after you read this, close your eyes. First, focus on your breath for a few inhales and exhales, then let yourself be the welcoming space for whatever sensations are appearing. Even if the sensations are very strong, let them be free to be here in whatever way they want to. And be so receptive that subtle sensations receive the invitation that they're welcomed in conscious awareness. If you notice that you're judging your experience or that you want it to change, welcome these tendencies as well. Continue welcoming sensations as long as you'd like to, until you feel the movement to open your eyes.

## The Liberation of Long-Held Emotions

The practice of opening to physical sensation is profound, partly because it's the medicine needed for the resolution of emotional pain. Emotions are a natural expression of being human, and how we experienced them early in life lays the foundation for how we hold them moving forward.

As children, our feelings needed just the unconditional welcoming that you're learning to give yourself now. But if the adults who took care of you denied your feelings or you were made to feel wrong for having them, by necessity you had to figure out what to do with them. Most of us push them underground, outside of awareness, where the physical energy stays undigested in the body, sometimes for decades. Meanwhile your attention goes into your mind, trying to make sense of your emotion-driven reactions and tendencies. This is how you come to think of yourself as worthless or unlovable. You reason that if you feel so bad, there must be something wrong with you.

Welcoming emotions begins to bring you back into balance. *Because presence is the peacemaker.* It liberates the energy that's been stuck in your body and dissolves the defenses that separate you from yourself. As you inhabit the space that by its nature welcomes all of your experience, you're effortlessly relaxed and whole instead of reactive and emotional.

Sometimes old, unexplored emotions feel like they're an expression of you from a younger age. There may be the fearful two-year-old afraid of his father's wrath or the neglected five-year-old who always focuses on pleasing everyone around her. As these emotions come to light, it can help to identify these unresolved parts of you as they relate to your history. My client Tanya became very familiar with the sad third-grader in her who couldn't tell anyone that her uncle was abusing her. Including the context for when the feeling arose helped her to know when it was present, so she could meet her experience of it with tremendous acceptance and compassion.

Emotions will reappear because that's what they do, but each time is fresh. Simply open fully to whatever comes. Can you feel how loving this is? There's nothing to change or fix—simply welcome everything unconditionally with absolute acceptance. The story eventually subsides, and you realize yourself more and more deeply— pure, untouched, and somehow mysteriously, fully alive.

Think of an emotion that arises frequently in you. Reflect within, and see if you can give this emotion an age, by simply asking, "How old are you?" Now practice welcoming the emotion with this added context.

## When You're Flooded by Emotions

I once worked with Maria, who showed great willingness to not be defined by the stories of her past life circumstances. But whenever she turned toward her feelings, she was immediately overwhelmed. The pain she began to recognize and feel into was so great that she just couldn't stay with it. She panicked and turned away in distress.

The ultimate healing of personal suffering is to realize that your essential nature is awareness itself. But our identities as separate people, with beliefs about who we are and the feelings that go with those beliefs, can be all-consuming. Grief, rage, terror, or sorrow—they occupy your mind space, take you over so you can't sleep, and leave you distraught and out of sorts. They may feel like they're too much to bear.

If this is the case for you, rather than bringing your attention right into welcoming these feelings directly, it may be useful to take some interim steps. These steps will help you begin to feel more comfortable with your emotional experience.

The goal of these practices is not to avoid the intensity of your feelings. Rather, they help you begin to ease into being present with them. If you're used to numbing out or avoiding, they invite you to experiment with being aware of your right-now reality in small doses and safe ways until you feel ready to meet the feelings directly.

Be flexible in how you use these practices. Do them if they help you, and let go of them altogether if and when they don't feel appropriate for you. They're merely suggestions—ways to play with your experience to incline your attention away from limiting identities and toward the freedom of your true nature.

## Conscious Breathing

The breath is a useful tool when you're overwhelmed by emotions. Taking deep, conscious breaths soothes the nervous system and brings space to contracted muscles in your torso. When your emotions feel out of control and your mind is full of churning thoughts, you'll discover the elegance of conscious breathing as a way into presence.

We've done this before, but why not try it again now? Close your eyes and put your attention on the sensations of breathing as you inhale and exhale. Exhale completely, then from your low belly, feel the ribs expand around your whole body as you inhale to fill your lungs with breath, then take your time to exhale. Make your exhale a little longer than your inhale. Inhale to a count of four or five, then exhale to a count of six or seven. If it feels helpful, place one had on your heart and one on your belly and take normal breaths in between each deep breath. There's no rush, so take your time with this.

Only if you feel ready, see where the breath can take you. Play with letting go of paying attention to the breath and become aware of any other physical sensations that might be present. Stay there for a few seconds, or longer if it feels okay. If this is scary for you, go back to focusing on the breath.

## Physical Soothing

Feelings can sometimes be too distressing to meet directly. When they are, give yourself some physical care. Hug yourself, or stroke your arm, neck, head, face, or shoulders. Focus on the physical sensations that occur as you do this. And you might even add some calming statements, such as "You'll get through this," or "You're okay."

Using this practice to turn down the volume on your experience of emotions prepares you to go deeper. Once you feel ready, expand your attention to the safe haven of being aware. Lovingly welcome whatever physical sensations are present as if you're welcoming a cherished part of yourself—because you are.

Now it's your turn to try it in your own unique way. What areas of your body are asking for physical soothing?

## Grounding in Your Environment

Sometimes it feels like too much to even bring any of your attention to your inner experience, so focus instead on your environment. When emotion overtakes you, start naming what you're perceiving through your senses—the air on my skin, birds chirping, trees moving in the wind, a table and chairs, and so on.

Or stand up and feel your feet firmly on the earth. Then take some conscious breaths or place your hands on your heart and belly and feel the connection with yourself. Notice what's coming in through your senses. Slowly name what you see, hear, taste, smell, or touch. Take your time with these exercises as you bring your attention to your present-moment experience.

Ready to try it so you know what it feels like?

## Orienting to Your Heart's Desire

Once you're aware that you're in a moment of turmoil, reflect on what you really want for this moment. How do you want this moment to be? Repeat whatever words resonate for you like a prayer—peace, calm, relaxation, steadiness, stillness.

With any of these practices, as the feeling of being overwhelmed subsides, begin to turn your attention toward the emotion. Emotions run through you, but they're not you. Do not focus on the story. Instead, drop your attention from your thoughts and bring awareness to your body. Be the receiving presence, with a heart so open that you welcome all sensations. Be fully in harmony with the moment—awake and aware as presence itself.

## Fear of Emotions

If you're like most people, you might fear the unexplored terrain of your emotions because you don't know what you will find. You recoil at certain strong sensations, or your mind starts spinning, making it hard to stay connected to the sensations in your body.

Fear is behind the pull to turn away from directly experiencing the sensations that come with feelings. And there are many reasons you might be afraid of actually turning toward and experiencing feelings. Here are some possibilities:

- You're petrified to meet what you've been avoiding for so long.

- You fear you're too weak to explore emotional pain.

- You're not confident in your ability be with your feelings.

- You're afraid you'll be overwhelmed and won't know what to do.

- If you turn toward the pain, you're afraid you'll cry forever.

- You're afraid of being uncomfortable.

Or maybe you believe you're justified in holding on to your feelings because you've been wronged by someone, or you're waiting for an apology that you think will make everything right.

All of these viewpoints are understandable. Difficult things happen in life, and feelings hurt, which is why we push them away. But if you give these fears power, you'll stay stuck in recycling your feelings. Here, in the spirit of freedom, I'm asking you to gently turn toward your emotions and welcome them, even if you're afraid of them. With great willingness and courage you allow yourself to feel what you've been avoiding for so long.

David grew up with a mother who was so depressed that she sometimes spent weeks in bed. His father was often out working, so he and his sister were left to fend for themselves. He remembers his mother looking him right in the eye with an intimate gaze that said to him, "I'm so depressed. I'm so sorry I'm putting this on you, but I can't help myself."

Now, decades later, David feels awkward making eye contact with almost everyone. He feels a strong urge to turn away, but he realizes that he is putting up a barrier to more intimate connections.

I placed a pillow on a chair facing him. I invited him to imagine that this was his mother, and I asked him to look at her and say whatever came up. The tendency to avoid was so strong! He could barely look at the pillow without a rush of sorrow and frustration arising in him. He had been resisting these feelings for a very long time.

We need to honor the tendencies to resist our emotions but not let these tendencies keep us from the peace we desire. This is why the first core practice, which invites you to turn toward your experience, is so essential. If you continue to avoid the direct experience of your feelings, nothing will change. You'll keep burying the pain while you're out in the world trying to find solutions—waiting for the person who will love you the way you long to be loved, waiting for the apology that doesn't come, or simply waiting for the pain to disappear.

When you make the decision to take the plunge and turn toward the shame and despair, you're taking control with the only action you can make. You can't change the past or make your feelings change, but you can control how you relate to your present-moment experience. You stop waiting and start to notice what you're experiencing. Why? Because it's here by grace and asking for your love and attention. You do what you can, which is to become exquisitely present with what is offered to you in the moment. You end the battle of separation by resisting what is true, and you say *Yes* to this—this breath, these sensations, the loving space of aware presence.

The invitation here is not to fight with the tendencies to avoid and resist. There is space for them, too, so welcome them. Welcome in a field of love the desire to turn away, the urge to close yourself off. Honor the wisdom of these tendencies trying to protect you; they arise in the field of awareness that needs no protection. Lay down the defenses, unearth what's been hidden in darkness, and let the stories crumble. Shine the laser light of awareness on what remains, and experience the infinite peace that's possible here and available in any moment.

Joy wrote on my blog, "For most of my life, I used to ignore/deny/bury any feelings that made me feel inadequate. I know this emotional pain resulted in physical pain. When I chose to heal past wounds, I began to acknowledge feelings as they surfaced and hold space for them until they pass…there is a natural flow that is peace-filled when I honor this process. Fear of a feeling gives it power to direct my steps, faith in a feeling allows me to fold it in and create with it. And the depth and heart opening that comes with Feeling All leaves me in wonder and gratitude."

Make a list of the reasons why you resist turning toward your feelings. With great kindness, go through each one and let it be present in you. Instead of going with the movement to resist, you're welcoming it. It's okay to feel scared as you explore feelings.

# Bringing Clarity and Intelligence to Your Experience

I never cease to be amazed by the fact that it's possible to find our way out of suffering—any time and in any moment. Suffering is not our true reality. It's a passing experience that is built on false ideas and distorted views of ourselves, others, and the world. What is real? *This*—the fullness of this alive presence vibrating with the energy of life.

Ultimately, realizing this freedom from limiting identities happens by grace when the mind is ready to let go. We can't make ourselves wake up to this reality, because the truth is realized only when any sense of a separate self falls away. There is no "I" here who can make anything happen, no doer—there is only consciousness that is the source of everything, empty of forms and overflowing with life.

But there is much you can do to lay the fertile ground for this realization. You can learn to work with your experience, which helps you to gain confidence in your ability to untangle yourself from conditioned identities. This is just what the core practices invite you to do. They show you how to embrace your inner experience with understanding and love.

If your desire to be liberated from the pain of unworthiness is strong, if you're fed up with the years of suffering, you'll stop blaming others or living in the belief that the world has dealt you a bad hand. When these thoughts arise, you welcome them fully as an opportunity to discover the peace that is already here. You notice stressful, self-denigrating thought patterns that derail your happiness, and you lose interest in them. You're caught in a tornado of feelings or the subtle buzz of anxiety, and you meet these experiences with deep acceptance. You constantly apply the tools and insights presented here to your in-the-moment experience because that's where the rubber meets the road.

Even if you feel stuck, paralyzed by the power of old conditioning, you can bring deep welcoming to this experience of being stuck—which begins to shift everything. Conditioned patterns of thinking and feeling arise—that's what they do, and you can't control the fact that they appear. But you can absolutely control what you do with them once they're here.

In any moment, you can choose how to meet your experience. You can stay mired in the old habitual patterns that take you farther from peace, or you can turn to what you're experiencing and say hello to the sadness, fear, and belief that you're deficient.

What do you choose in this moment?

Steve commented on my blog about the fierce desire for freedom. He related that he was in a relationship with someone who had caused him a lot of pain over the years. Choosing not to walk away from this person, he wrote: "Every time I feel angry or pushed away, I stay as aware as possible of my own experience and feel the physical sensations. I witness the story, learn the lesson, and let go of it. I have enough experience to know that stories make it worse. I'm always making a choice: Do I want to harbor resentment or do I want to be totally peaceful? I choose peace by letting the story go and feeling the sensations."

See how he embodies the core practices? Every time he's hurting, he turns toward his experience, realizes he is aware, loses interest in stories, and welcomes physical sensations. It isn't always easy, but it's the choice he makes over and over, and it brings him peace.

Choosing how you meet your experience is a fundamental stepping-stone to the ultimate freedom, which is knowing the truth of who you are. This understanding, which we'll clarify in the next chapter, puts to rest the belief in any separate, personal identity. You come to know that you are one with this loving presence. Without your personal identity, troublesome beliefs just don't hold water and emotions have nowhere to land. Knowing yourself as your true nature, there's nothing to defend and no one who lacks anything. In fact, this is already who you are—and you get to know this intimately.

## Summary

This chapter introduced core practice #4: welcoming feelings with love and acceptance. We learned that what we call an emotion or feeling is made up of a story line in our thoughts and physical sensations that appear in the body. The core practice of welcoming invites us to rest our attention in the space of being aware, which, by its nature, welcomes all physical sensations. The body holds unexplored emotions from the past in the form of physical contractions—until these contractions are met in the loving space of awareness. Welcoming ends the division with our own experience, so we can relax with what is. We no longer need to hide, avoid, pretend, or deny.

Sometimes emotions are too strong to welcome directly. Several practices were suggested to use with overwhelming emotions, including conscious breathing, physical soothing, grounding in your environment, and orienting to your heart's desire. These practices prepare you to fully be with the direct experience of emotions as they appear in the body.

In the next chapter we'll explore core practice #5: the sacred return. We'll discover the natural, unnameable, all-encompassing reality that just is, our true home, where the suffering of separation ends.

# CHAPTER 7

# CORE PRACTICE #5: THE SACRED RETURN

Give your attention to the experience
of seeing rather than to the object seen
and you will find yourself everywhere.

—Rupert Spira

I knew Peggy from the many retreats we both attended over the years. She was always friendly, but I could tell from our interactions that she was unsure of herself. Every time we spoke she chattered nonstop, and I felt an underlying anxiety—even a frantic quality—in her.

The last time I saw her, she seemed distinctly different. She was deeply quiet, clearly relaxed; she spoke less quickly, and she embodied the space to listen and reflect while we talked. I knew that something profound had shifted in her. When I brought up what I noticed, she briefly referred to a newfound inner knowing, and I could tell she didn't want to say more. I suspect that her belief in the structures of her identity and personality—what we call "Peggy"—had fallen away, along with anxiety and the need to fill space with words. The peace was palpable.

The sacred return happens when conscious awareness frees itself from the tangle of conditioned thoughts and feelings. Your life is no longer built around the personal identity made up of memories, judgments, needs, and expectations. These arise, but you know they don't define you. With your attention now free, you begin to get a taste of the light of your true nature, which is consciousness, the boundless and pure life energy that animates all things. You may not realize it, but at some level you know this aliveness already! It's what breathes you and underlies every moment of your existence.

The exploration of consciousness invites us to go beyond conventional psychology, which tries to fix the personal self, and to look deeply into the spiritual dimension of life. It's the only real solution I know to human suffering—to know who we are not and who we are.

Discovering that who you are is consciousness itself is a lifelong journey for many. The mind has to be ready to crack open, and this is something we can't ultimately control. It helps a lot if you make what I'm offering here as real as possible in your own experience. Don't just take in the words. Stop often, close your eyes, and be fully present to what's here right now, the sense of presence outside of your thoughts and feelings. You're not looking for a thought that will make everything right. Relax away from all thought and you'll begin to tap into this essential aliveness.

As we've seen, the thinking mind grips strongly, so you need to notice when thoughts have taken hold. Your fire for freedom will serve you well as you continually apply the core practices to your in-the-moment experience. But things also work in mysterious ways. I've seen people struggle with awakening to their true nature while failing to notice that they're already less stressed, more relaxed, and better able to enjoy life. Since you've read this far in the book as we've untangled the personal identity, I suspect you're reaping the benefits, even if you don't consciously realize it.

My client Melanie stayed agitated for the first eighteen months of our work together, but we kept at it. Almost out of the blue, peace became her priority. She cherished this peace and began to make decisions that supported it. She interacted less with toxic people in her life and made her work situation less demanding. She became way more in touch with her loving and caring nature, letting it shine more openly in her everyday life.

Notice the thoughts and feelings that bring you suffering and apply the core practices to dispel them. And always return to the most important part of your present-moment experience. This is what's real: the boundless experience of being aware. Keep returning your attention here, over and over. Start to recognize when you don't feel as scared or needy as you used to. Be aware when the moments of stillness, happiness, and peace appear.

The sacred return is not a change, a movement, a transformation, or an action that makes you more peaceful. You don't become something or someone different than you are. *It is simply a conscious realization of what is already true*—knowing the life force that is the underlying source of everything. And knowing that this life force is who you are.

You think yourself into being a person who is undeserving and destined to be unhappy. But when consciousness awakens to itself as the source of all, it is known, beyond a shadow of a doubt, that "you" are not this limited, separate person who lacks, strives, needs, and defends. Every cell of your being knows that you are the infinite awareness not separate from anything. Finally you are free of the beliefs that diminish your happiness and squash your joy and creative spirit. Life is now gloriously free to express itself through you without limitation.

How does this realization happen? "You," as your separate self with a name and life story, don't realize anything. Rather, the mind structures that create this sense of a separate "you" collapse, dissolve, or fall away. You awaken from the dream of your personal identity. Consciousness, no longer attached to personal thoughts and feelings, makes the sacred return home to itself.

When you know who you truly are, you realize that you are, and always have been, effortlessly aware and at ease. Even while you've been out in the world, functioning as a person who is inadequate and unworthy, this stillness has been here, but you haven't been aware of it. This pure you is untouched by the events of your life. It experiences them, but like a drama played out on a stage. You know that those events do not define you, because they're not the reality of you. While you've been busy living those stories and wanting things to be different than they are, you've simply overlooked this timeless peace.

## Discovering Infinite Awareness

You *know* this truth because it is the reality of who you are. It is the silence at the heart of all sounds, the stillness from which movement arises. But many people struggle to know this experience consciously because, as we know, the familiar mind structures that create the sense of separation are very powerful.

Ultimately, words fail to portray the limitless, profound peace and happiness that is your true nature. We're trying to describe in words what can only be known by direct experiencing. Say that you've never eaten an apple, and your friend is trying to explain to you what it tastes like. He'll tell you that it is crispy, juicy, and sweet, but until you take that first bite, you won't really know the taste. You might imagine it or pretend you know it, but for you to truly understand the joy of eating a delicious apple, you need to experience it directly.

Just like in this example, I'll be using words to describe what can only be experienced. But what I'll be describing is not an object like an apple. It's so much closer than that because it is who you already are. It's the overlooked experience of yourself prior to any identity, which is formless, infinite, and totally at peace.

Say that you forgot that years ago you ate an apple. Your friend tries to describe it to you, and you can't quite get it. Then you take a bite and the memory reawakens. You exclaim, "Oh, yes! I know this taste." Directly experiencing your true nature is like that. When it is consciously realized, you are remembering what is already true.

As you read the descriptions below, open your mind, your body, your heart, and every aspect of your being. What's most important is not the words themselves, but what is transmitted through and between the words. Just like words that describe the taste of an apple, these words point to what you can only know directly: the intimate experience of you beyond any limited identities. Don't use your mind to chew on any concepts. Relax and be open to the stillness from which these words arise.

Each description includes an exploration to help you get a taste of the underlying truth about reality. Let yourself be fully absorbed in presence, and return here again and again. Stay curious, and if you start struggling, move on to another exploration. Most importantly, enjoy the process!

## What Is Real?

All things in life appear and disappear. Thoughts change, feelings come and go like weather, and our life situations are constantly evolving. See if this is true for you. Are you always feeling the same way? Does your view of things change?

### Consciousness Is Ever Present

If the things of the world aren't stable, then what's real? Although thoughts, feelings, situations, and even relationships seem real at the time they're present, there's something unreal about them if they can change so readily. They're not lasting, and you can't rely on them. And if you stake your happiness on things that change, you certainly can't be assured of being happy. If all you know is the world of objects, you're left anxious about what could come or what could go at any moment.

So are you resigned to striving for happiness and hopefully getting it from time to time?

The only "thing" that is real is consciousness, the aliveness at the core of all things. It's not an object, and it doesn't come and go. It is the full-on, undeniable immediacy of aware presence, life itself as it is right now, formless, free of content, and ever present. Here, there's no personal identity and no resistance to anything. This is peace, and this peace, unlike the objects of the world, is completely reliable.

In the moments when you release attention from the contents of the mind, your allegiance shifts to this formless space of presence. You're no longer batted about by the comings and goings of thoughts—and you're at peace. It's like you've realized you're the vast and open sky, and you're undisturbed by any clouds that might float through.

## Freedom from Conditioning

The core practices are designed to unravel the personal beliefs that you're inadequate and unlovable. They show you that these thoughts and feelings aren't real—they're not the absolute truth of who you are. And when you know what isn't real, you're poised for the amazing discovery of your boundless, peaceful true nature.

It's a moment to celebrate when you see a familiar thought pattern starting to grab you, and you just don't take it on. You stay stable in the knowing that this is not who you are. This is what happened to my client Ruth, who lived with a very strong inner critic. In our work together, she identified this inner voice, felt the effects of it, and brainstormed ways to deal with it. Slowly Ruth began to feel happier overall, and then one day she realized that she didn't have to listen to this voice anymore—it no longer defined her. So liberating!

Using the core practices, you:

🌀 Turn toward your inner experience.

🌀 Become aware of what you're experiencing.

🌀 Understand the nature of thoughts and thinking, and lose interest in the content of your thoughts.

🌀 Know that the essence of emotions is the physical sensations you experience, and welcome these sensations in the arms of loving awareness.

Together, these practices soften the hold of the identity as a separate self, which is the one who feels lacking and inadequate. They take you out of the web of your conditioning and open you to what is true. Seeing the objects that arise in you as temporary and changeable and not absolutely real takes you to the threshold of discovering this all-encompassing peace—empty of objects and so incredibly alive.

Think of a recent time when you experienced an unpleasant emotional reaction. Go through the first four core practices, applying them to this experience. Now play with settling your attention in the field of awareness in which objects arise. Close your eyes and don't think about or look for anything. Just be—open to the pure aliveness that's here, the sense of peace that comes from being one with what is.

Your imagination may help you. Imagine what it would be like to have no sense of separation with anything. You're not contracted into a body—the essence of who you are is everywhere.

## The Shift from Doing to Being

As a separate self, we assume that if we're not okay as we are, then something needs to change. We need to get what we think we're missing or to fix what is broken. We try to stop thoughts, manage feelings, control others, and change our circumstances so we can finally find the ease we're looking for. It feels like we're human doings, not human beings.

All these actions—getting, fixing, trying, searching—are functions of the separate self. And they only serve to separate us from our true nature. They impel us to look outside of our own experience and into our minds or out into the world to find the objects that we hope will fulfill us. Can you feel the pressure of all this doing in your own mind and body?

## Effortless Being

I have great news for you. Your true nature, which is already who you are, is full and complete in itself. It's effortlessly here and alive without you doing anything. In fact, when your focus is all on the effort of doing, you're bound to miss this underlying quiet, effortless experience of being.

Who you are is not an object to be attained, and you don't realize who you are by using your mind to solve the question of your identity. What happens is that the illusion of separation dissolves and you, as consciousness, realize what is already true—that your true identity expands way beyond the idea of you as a separate self. The separate self is a doer, whereas consciousness just is.

Can you feel into the implications of this truth? You, as a separate self, assume that you'll be unsuccessful if you stretch beyond your comfort zone. You shut down a creative idea before it even begins to come alive in you. But you, as consciousness, have no such limits. You are overflowing with potential, completely undefended and open to everything. You're fully available to accept, welcome, love, appreciate, and be.

In the moments when the idea of the separate self falls away and pure being is known and experienced, problems dissolve. Without a separate self, there's no story line that you think defines you. There's no one who can be hurt by another, no one who takes things personally, and no one who feels inadequate and unworthy. Here, nothing needs to be changed or improved, because there is just the felt experience of the fullness of life unfolding. Without doing anything, you're alert, awake, completely at peace, and problem-free.

## Awakened Action

At the core of being, your true nature is the infinite space of silence and stillness. But doing still happens. You have the capacity to choose actions and the body has the capacity to carry them out. Just look at the world! We raise our children, brush our teeth, go to work, take a walk in the woods. We build skyscrapers and cross oceans. Even though the absolute truth of things is the underlying field of awareness that is pure being with no forms in it, we function in the human life with an unfathomable diversity of actions.

Actions coming from separation are born of a sense of fear and lack. They aren't taken simply for the joy of living this human life. They're made with a goal in mind—to fulfill a need or improve a situation. They're designed to protect your sense of worth or please others so that you are sure to get their approval.

But actions coming from being are free and uncaused. They emerge from stillness as an expression of the undivided truth of this now moment. They come simply from joy, compassion, intelligence, appreciation of beauty, or the call of the current situation.

Are you steeped in fear and ruled by lack? Or are you open and free? You might show up in an interaction suppressing yourself because you're afraid of being judged or fearful that you won't be listened to. And what's your experience? There's a track of thoughts in your mind that makes you feel separate.

Now imagine showing up open, curious, grateful, not needing anything, letting the conversation flow where it will. With no need to protect or defend, there's no agenda. You're listening, responding, feeling compassion and understanding—just being.

## Practices Help

Practices, including the first four core practices presented in this book, seem to contain an element of doing. There may be a sense of someone who turns toward inner experience or welcomes sensations—and these actions may be very helpful. This is how the mind and personal intention serve awakening to your true nature.

The paradox is that in the end, you can't awaken yourself from the trance of separation because what you realize is that there's no "you" who does the awakening. You may practice, as the Buddha said, like your hair is on fire, you may rest in effortless contentment, or anywhere in between. Regardless of what you do, who you are is and always has been the silence of being reflected everywhere.

Think of a situation that triggers you, and find the sense of lack or fear that drives you. Feel into the personal doer who wants to control and fix the situation. Now imagine coming from pure being that is already whole and needs nothing. You're just here as openness, with no fear, lack, or agenda. The moment feels so fresh! Reflect on these questions:

- How do you look at the situation now?

- How do you experience your body and mind?

- How do you experience the other people involved?

- What do you feel moved to do or say from this loving place free of conditioning?

## *Beyond Time*

Suffering always has to do with thoughts about the past and future, but if you're suffering, it's happening now. Look closely and you'll see that there is no such thing as the past or future. You can ruminate about the past and what should have been—but you're doing that now. You can worry about the future and all the scary things that might happen—but you're doing that now. When the "future" comes, when are you experiencing it? Now. And "now" is not a slice in time. It's infinite, expansive being, uncontained by time or space.

## In the Now

The mind is pulled into thoughts about the past and future, and these distract you from experiencing present-moment aliveness. When you completely lose interest in the content of thoughts, the sense of separation dissolves, and immediately you're home, here as the light of your true nature.

What time is it? Always now. What's present in timelessness? You, free of any personal identity and one with life.

With your attention immersed in presence and not in thoughts, suffering is impossible. Amazing! There's no "one" here to suffer.

But there is a movement of pure being that seems to want to manifest itself in the world of forms and objects. We seem to be in a human body, in relationship to others, managing the comings and goings of life, celebrating birth and mourning loss. We change and grow, and our life situations evolve. Time seems to be very real.

How do we reconcile this paradox? How is it possible that reality is empty of time and form when objects in time seem to be our reality?

I first heard this teaching about the timeless and formless nature of reality at a retreat many years ago. Shortly afterward, I was kayaking on a beautiful stretch of river, moving gently with the current. I began to observe some birds on the shore using their long pointy beaks designed to dig into the sand in just the right way to find tiny crabs to eat. I was amazed by the perfection of this scene before me and couldn't grasp how these beautiful forms weren't real.

What I understand now is that all forms emerge as temporary expressions of the life force. As each form is seen clearly for what it actually is, it shines with the light of its source—consciousness. That certainly was the case for the birds I was watching. I saw the forms and they seemed real. But seeing through them to the beauty and perfection of the moment showed me what was actually real. The forms were perceived and had a certain reality to them, but their source was known as pure awareness.

## Experiencing Life Without Attachment

The implications of this understanding are transformative for human life. We enjoy and appreciate the things of the world, but we're not attached to them. We feel the array of emotions fully without getting caught in their drama. We don't have to take things personally, which leaves open the possibility of responding with endless compassion.

We experience an exquisite tenderness as we meet life in all its forms. We understand and feel for the confusion we witness in people who are defined by their thoughts and belief systems. And we live fully in the now without being held back by ideas about the nonexistent past or future.

Live this truth and your heart can't help but overflow. The veils of lack and separation thin, and you're here, seeing yourself in everything—innocent, open, luminous, and free.

Go out into nature, and find a place to sit quietly. Choose one object and contemplate it deeply.

- Realize that in this moment there is no past or future.

- See this object as a temporary expression of the life force, the source of all things, including yourself.

> ✣ See through the form of the object and contact its source—the luminous nature of pure awareness shining through it.
>
> ✣ Feel the sense of nonseparation.

## Perfectly Natural

Life in all its forms arises as a perfectly natural unfolding, regardless of whether the conscious mind is aware of it or not. Pure aware presence is never in conflict with anything.

### Consciousness Accepts Everything

Any thought, perception, or emotion can appear in you, and awareness has no problem with it. The worst terror you could imagine? An outpouring of grief? Guilt, shame, jealousy, disappointment, or despair? The formless space of being aware doesn't judge, fight, or resist any of it. Why? Because every form arises from the one source. Be that source, awareness, and you'll know that everything, in its essence, is you.

Can you imagine the ocean rejecting a wave or expecting it to be different than it is? There is just the ebb and flow of forms arising and passing away in an underlying current of everything being at ease with what is.

### Easeful Flow

Study nature to understand this easeful flow. There are no mistakes. Seeds land where they do, and trees grow. Wind blows and branches sway. Flowers bloom. Birds nest. There is no conflict or resistance in the natural world, and knowing your natural state as openhearted awareness means that you get to live this easeful flow.

But add in the human mind, and things get sticky. If your vantage point is stories, emotions, and limited ideas about yourself and the world, you'll contract into separation, and you'll suffer. Knowingly be awareness at the heart of everything, and you're one with the unfolding of life, not resisting anything.

At the end of a day, take some time to reflect on the things you did. You got out of bed, took a shower, put on some clothes, ate breakfast, drove to work, and so on. As you look back on the day, notice how many things happened without your mind being involved. Even if the mind produced a running commentary, these actions would still have happened whether or not you were thinking.

Reflect on the fact that there is a flow to life that unfolds without the intervention of your personal sense of self.

Now go outside and take a look at a tree. Realize that without any effort of any kind, the seed sprouted, leaves grew, and the tree is here moving in the wind.

Contemplate that there is a perfectly natural way that life unfolds that has very little to do with the content of our minds. Take out a piece of paper and write about this question: How can I get out of the way of this unfolding and let it happen?

## Empty and Full

This being-aware experience can be described as being both empty and full. It's the formless state of pure being, so it's empty of all separate forms. Although the world is full of forms, awareness itself is formless. There are no objects—no stories, thoughts, needs, preference, or emotion. There's no confusion or anxiety, no judgments or expectations, no time or space, and not even the sensation of the breath. It's like a mirror with nothing reflected in it—clear, timeless, open space.

This is you—pure emptiness.

## Full of Life

And the deepest stillness realized when forms fall away is also incredibly full and alive. It's overflowing with life, the movement of life, pure aliveness. It's bright and luminous and holds unlimited potential for anything, way beyond what the mind can imagine or envision.

When the being-aware experience of your true nature is forgotten, you're filled with ideas based on the limited, inadequate sense of self and thoughts that pull you into thinking about the past and future. It's like you're acting a role in a play, and the script has already been written. There's no space for anything fresh and new outside this mind-set.

## Knowing Who You Are

Untangle from these thoughts, and you'll wake up to awareness that is empty of stressful objects and full of gratitude and enthusiasm. See if you can feel into this potential.

Here, the idea of personal lack seems almost like a joke. With an undeniable knowing that everything is you, you're so magnificently full, with your heart tender, open, and sometimes bursting with joy and celebration.

Nothing is resisted or felt to be wrong or missing, so you realize you're one with life. You experience stillness, ease, and peace greater than you could imagine. Physical tensions are met as they appear, with no interest in the mental activity it takes to make something of them. Everything is ordinary because there is the illusion of familiar forms—but extraordinary in the awe of its very existence.

Can you taste it?

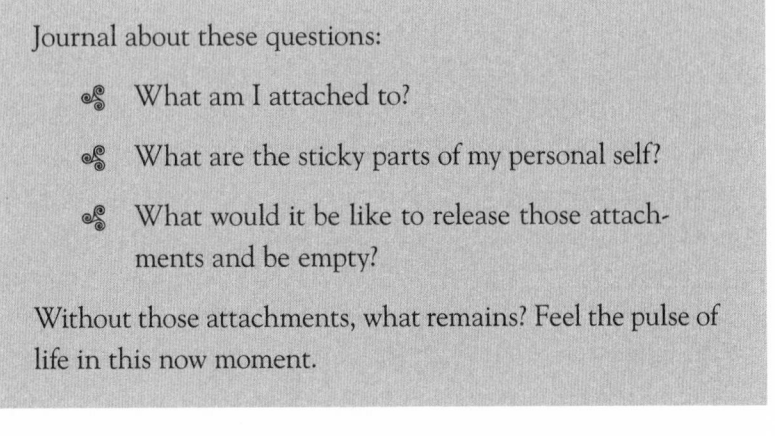

Journal about these questions:

- What am I attached to?

- What are the sticky parts of my personal self?

- What would it be like to release those attachments and be empty?

Without those attachments, what remains? Feel the pulse of life in this now moment.

## Living Nondual Awareness

My client Natalie was very involved with her church and thought of herself as a spiritual person. She attended the service every Sunday and participated in several committees. She desperately wanted to be happy and tried her best to live the teachings she learned in church. But she was frustrated. None of her personal relationships lasted. She felt extremely judgmental toward the men she dated and easily provoked into anger. Ashamed of her behavior but unable to control it, she felt she didn't deserve God's love. She was confused about how to make the religious teachings her living reality.

Knowing your true nature as infinite presence is not a secret teaching or lofty ideal. It's not about pretending that you're spiritual, following religious doctrine, or coming up with new age notions about how you're supposed to be. It's the living, breathing reality of this life as it's appearing right now, coming through you.

It's about taking off all blinders and seeing things as they are. It's about questioning all ideas to get to the core truth and being willing to explore what it's like to live according to this truth. It's about meeting the juicy experience of life in whatever way it shows up. This is what Natalie was being called to discover.

You get to live this truth as it unfolds in you when you've surrendered to its grace. And you get to see how conditioning derails you from peace. You get to be emotional, triggered, messy, and sublimely confused—experiencing the range of human reactions. You get to forget who you are, then remember once again. And none of this negates the essential truth—that you are pure being itself.

Opening to everything from the endless space of being aware offers a life that is so rich! You get to live—truly, madly, deeply. You feel what's here without skipping over any of it, and you let your exploration of objects show you the way to the bare truth of this now moment.

The next two sections are devoted to living the truth of nondual awareness. You can consciously live this truth right now, getting out of the way and letting things unfold in perfect harmony with life.

## Revisiting the Guiding Principles and Core Practices

As you know by now, the four guiding principles are the wake-up call that interrupts the mind-set of suffering and reminds you of what is true—about the conditioned patterns that take you over and the nature of nondual reality. Know that you can embody these principles—that is, you can make them real in your own experience, in any moment.

1.  The identity of "I am not enough" is made up of distorted thoughts that view the self, others, and the world through a lens that is limited and false.

2.  No matter how real it seems, the identity of unworthiness is optional. You don't have to be defined by it.

In light of what you now know to be true, can you feel how the limited identity you take to be you is becoming more transparent?

Can you see how you are at least a little more open to the possibility that it doesn't actually define you?

3. You have control over shifting your attention to different parts of your experience.

4. There is more to your experience in any moment than your thoughts and feelings.

Can you find the fundamental aliveness right here in the moment beyond thought?

Now let's revisit the five core practices in light of what you now know about finding your true home as awareness.

Think of a way that your beliefs about yourself and others distract you from being happy. Maybe you blame yourself when things go wrong or you feel lost and undeserving when others don't include you. Maybe you easily go into a whirlwind of self-criticism.

We're using your story line as a starting point, but the content of the story doesn't matter. The practices are applicable any time a hint of a personal identity has taken hold.

Notice that if you go along as you always have, believing your story, you will stay in this familiar conditioned reaction and be unavailable to the natural flow of consciousness. You're involved in the content of your thoughts, creating a narrative about yourself, others, and the situation, and you're trapped in experiencing painful emotions.

Realizing that you're in a moment where you're believing limited thoughts about yourself, you stop and take a breath. Even this simple act is revolutionary, because immediately your nervous systems starts to calm and you remember that another way is possible:

🌀 You turn toward your experience with openness, curiosity, self-compassion, and the dedication to know what's true.

❀ Centering your attention in the space of being aware, you notice the thoughts and feelings that make you suffer.

❀ You lose interest in the content of thoughts.

❀ You lovingly welcome any physical sensations that are present.

❀ Then you are poised to discover the vast space beyond thought that is stable, alive, unmoving, and completely at peace with itself.

I've probably called upon these practices tens of thousands of times over the years. And each time is joyful. Why? Because, as I said earlier, the magic is in the moment.

I never think *Oh, I've already dealt with that, but it still returned,* or *That feeling should be gone by now.* I don't judge, evaluate, or analyze my experience, and I don't compare it to what was or should be. I don't put myself down, thinking I've done something wrong because conditioned patterns arise again.

I take it as it comes, without a ripple, opening to the freedom available in this now moment.

Revisit the guiding principles and core practices whenever they're called for. For extra support, I have created a guided meditation that goes through them, which you can find at http:www .newharbinger.com/40156. Be enthusiastic and diligent in your quest for truth, as you relax and flow in harmony with presence.

## Living the Qualities of Being

In the moments when presence is well established and conditioning has faded into the background, there is spaciousness to celebrate life's treasures. The conscious realization of what's absolutely true crumbles the trance of your personal self and reveals lovely qualities that arise naturally in the knowing of pure being.

But you don't need to wait for the clouds to part to start noticing that these qualities already permeate your life experience. And you're welcome to live as if they were true—because they are.

## Peace

In the absence of all resistance, peace is your abiding experience. This peace is masked when you're at war with your inner experience. Something happens or a feeling arises, and you want to avoid it or change it, or you wish it would disappear.

As the attachment to thoughts falls away, an all-encompassing acceptance of all things as they are naturally appears, along with the deepest, most indescribable peace.

## Happiness

With nothing to resist, you're suddenly problem-free. The idea of problems may arise again, but, knowing that the magic is in the moment, you apply the core practices and realize the possibility of freedom.

We all so desperately want to be happy. And that happiness is here and available to be lived. Once the separate self is seen through, happiness is here—naturally. We can say that it is uncaused happiness. It doesn't come from objects or situations. It's the abiding state of your true nature.

## Wonder

Not using the mind to know, plan, or figure out, we're left in awe and wonder. Things are seen freshly, as if for the first time. And each time *is* the first time from the perspective of the timelessness of aware presence. Memories come only from the mind. But in the pure reality of things, we're continually touched and amazed.

We start to notice unfathomable coincidences, and we're rendered speechless by the tender beauty that life creates. At one with all, every single expression is a miracle.

## Intelligence

There is a naturally occurring intelligence of life that is far greater than the human mind. We can see it at work in nature. How could that bird's beak be designed in just the right way to find the perfect morsel of food? How could Beethoven have written such gorgeous symphonies—most of which were composed when he was deaf?

And we see it in the everyday events of life—watching children learn how things work, trying to comprehend the technology available at our fingertips, putting ingredients together to make a delicious dish, acknowledging the fact that we even have a face to wash. Our world is so complex! And it is an expression of the creative force of life that underlies everything.

This natural intelligence is so much more trustworthy than the mind. Surrendering the reliance on the mind leaves you in the space of not knowing and invites you into deep listening. You don't need to know what decision to make. You don't need to have a situation all figured out. You don't even need to know what to do or say next.

There is a core inner knowing that just knows—if you are willing to listen to it. See how you're called to act. See where you're moved to go. This aliveness is unconditioned and knows that everything is you. It can be fully trusted.

## Gratitude and Appreciation

Everyone knows we're supposed to be grateful, but from the perspective of awakened awareness, gratitude isn't a practice or a value. It's what arises naturally from knowing that nothing is separate from you. You end up living in gratitude.

This knowing naturally guides you to make the loving response that considers everyone and everything. You tread with care, appreciating the interconnectedness of all things.

## Enthusiasm

The mind interferes with zest for life. Without the droning mental commentary, what remains is enthusiasm for what's here in this moment. The word "enthusiasm" originates from the Greek meaning "inspired" or "possessed by a god."

Consciousness awake to itself is fully inspired by the moment and possessed by life! Forgetting memory, we invest fully in the experience of now, flowing with what arises. We feel fresh, innocent, eager, and amazed.

> Be on the lookout for the seeds of these naturally occurring qualities of awakened consciousness:
>
> - Peace
> - Happiness
> - Wonder
> - Intelligence
> - Gratitude and appreciation
> - Enthusiasm
>
> When you experience these qualities, look beyond the object or situation that seems to have triggered them and be fully alive in your in-the-moment experience. Relax into a taste of your true nature.

## Summary

The sacred return is the fifth core practice. The ultimate in finding freedom from feeling unworthy and unlovable, it is the conscious realization of the nondual nature of reality. It's not a change, a movement, or an action that makes you more peaceful. It is simply the conscious knowing of what is already true. You see through the veil of limited and personal identities and realize your true nature— the luminous presence beyond thought that is awake and alive in this now moment.

The sacred return is knowing yourself as conscious awareness. I offered these pointers, inviting you to discover them in your own experience:

- Your true nature is not an object that comes and goes.

- Knowing your true nature, you shift from doing to being.

- Reality is beyond time.

- It is perfectly natural.

- It is both empty and full.

Nondual awareness is not a spiritual concept—it's the living, breathing experience of reality as it is right now. In that sense, it is the stillness that gives rise to your everyday life. How do you embody nondual awareness?

- Be alive to your immediate experience by applying the four guiding principles and five core practices in moments of confusion, and

- Live the naturally occurring qualities of being: peace, happiness, wonder, intelligence, gratitude, and enthusiasm.

We've now concluded Part 1 of this book. I laid out the foundation of the guiding principles and core practices that help you find freedom from the painful identities of lack and unworthiness. These principles and practices help you to know the absolute truth—the boundless freedom that is your true nature. Now you are beginning to know, in your own experience, that suffering is truly optional.

In Part 2 you'll learn skills and perspectives to discover a better relationship with your past, to figure out how to not take things personally, and how to live from love and not fear. I'm excited to be delving into these topics with you!

# PART 2

# LIVING FREE

# CHAPTER 8

# A FRESH RELATIONSHIP WITH YOUR PAST

*Nothing ever happened in the past that can
prevent you from being present now.*

—Eckhart Tolle

One lovely afternoon I was enjoying a conversation with two friends who came for a visit from out of town. We were sitting at the pool area of a hotel when we realized we were all reacting to the scene unfolding in front of us. A little girl, about age four, was in front of an iPad, with Mom next to her absorbed in a magazine and Dad sitting two chairs away from Mom turned away and lost in his own thoughts. You could feel the disconnection among them.

In the pool were several children, most with a parent, who were playing and laughing together. The little girl on the chair stared wistfully at the kids in the pool, so desperately wanting to join in, while her parents were completely oblivious to her desires. It broke our hearts to recognize that at such a young age she was sadly resigned to her fate. If this was her everyday experience, and we suspected it was, how could she not develop false ideas about herself, relationships, and her place in the world?

Painful experiences like this one feed into the development of our personal and limiting identities. What do you think this little girl learned? I'm guessing, but I imagine she felt invisible and powerless. Taking on these identities, she is shut down from experiencing her natural aliveness. Can you feel how the life force was present in her natural wish to join the other kids in play—but deflated by her inability to do so?

Can you think of ways in which the life force in you has somehow been deflated?

As infants and young children, we're impressionable and eager to learn, so the messages we receive from how we're treated by others have a powerful effect on us. Unfortunately, the early experiences we have in life often set us up to believe that we are inadequate, lacking, and somehow not whole.

Carrying around the past means that you're living according to your conditioned reactions and rejecting the full reality of the present moment. The past isn't the problem. It's how the familiar, unexplored patterns that come from past experiences live in your mind and body now. This is what keeps you from consciously knowing the aliveness of your true nature.

As we all know, our thoughts about the past can stick like glue. In this chapter, you'll gain the tools you need to find freedom from conditioned ideas about your past. We'll cover how ruptures in your early relationships feed your sense of separation, the strategies of people pleasing and attention seeking that are the hallmark of the feeling of unworthiness, how you hold on to the past, and the meaning of forgiveness. All along, I'll encourage you to apply these new insights to your in-the-moment experience.

# How We Learn Not to Trust

The conditioned identities we hold about ourselves develop mostly from our early relationships. We can understand how this works by taking a look at attachment theory, which was formulated by psychologist John Bowlby (1988) in the mid- to late twentieth century and further refined by his colleague Mary Ainsworth. Their works describe how patterns are laid down in us as a result of our early experiences with our parents. These are learned patterns that operate mostly outside of conscious awareness and bring us suffering without our knowing why or how. If you feel afraid of being vulnerable with others or if you feel that those close to you won't be interested in what's important to you, these are signs of ruptures in early attachments. We bring light to these relationship dynamics not to blame or accuse anyone, but to help you untangle from conditioned ideas about yourself that limit your happiness.

The research of Dr. Ainsworth and colleagues (1978) with one- and two-year-olds revealed different attachment styles depending on the relationship between the children and their mothers. What defines the style of attachment is whether or not the mother was a consistent presence in the child's life and how attuned the mother was to her child's emotions. When these young children were securely attached, they could tolerate being with an unfamiliar person when the mother left the room, and they were happy and connected when the mother returned. The child's sense of trust meant that she was left with no emotional residue from her mother's absence.

In contrast, children who were insecurely attached showed fear when the mother left, avoidance of the mother when she returned, or mixed reactions such as clinging, anger, passivity, or giving up. Some were difficult to comfort.

Without going into all the details of this seminal research, what it reveals are the effects of ruptures in trust in early relationships. If you had parents who were controlling, distant, preoccupied, or absent—if you were physically, emotionally, or sexually abused—if traumatic situations occurred early on, such as death, divorce, or hospitalizations—these things leave their mark if they remain unresolved. You're left without understanding how to know and be with your own emotions, and confused about how to make authentic connections with others.

Through the veil of this mistrust, life appears to be scary, empty, and withholding, while its truth as being generous and infinitely loving is overlooked. As a result of these early unprocessed experiences, you may be locked into an identity of feeling unworthy and incapable. You just don't believe that you matter.

Recognizing the quality of your early attachments and how they affect you now can spotlight subtle aspects of conditioning. These are behaviors and mind-sets that feel so much like "you" that you don't realize they're not the true essence of who you are. And the emotions that drive them are hidden outside of conscious awareness.

At the end of one of my sessions with Mimi, she told me that she needed to cancel our next appointment. I nodded my head and deleted the appointment from my calendar without fanfare. Suddenly, with panic in her voice, she leaned forward and blurted out, "Is that okay? Do you mind that I need to cancel?"

Somehow Mimi had become so sensitive to disappointing others that she learned to intensely scan their reactions for approval. And when she didn't perceive this approval in my demeanor, she felt she had done something terribly wrong. This reaction, which Mimi told me happened often, made me wonder how many times she was dismissed during her early years when her own needs displeased her parents—and how painful that must have been for her.

For this exercise, I'm asking you to reflect on your early experiences in life. Some of us had a tough go of it, so be gentle with yourself, and if this exercise feels like too much, please skip it.

Take your time with these questions, and revisit them as often as you like. Feel free to write your reflections in a journal. Looking back at your first relationships,

- What did they feel like?

- Were they reliable and secure?

- Were there any breaks in trust, where you somehow learned that you couldn't rely on others for comfort and support?

- How did your parents respond to you when you were sad or afraid?

- From these experiences, what did you learn about yourself, others, and the world?

Now, as an adult,

- How have these relationships affected you?

- What patterns were laid down in these early relationships that bring you suffering now?

- What relationship do you have with your own emotions?

## Using the Principles and Practices

Recognizing the effects of early attachment problems in the moments when they arise offers an excellent opportunity to bring forth the guiding principles and the core practices. Let's walk through these with Mimi to see how it's possible for her to find her way out of this moment of suffering.

First, she takes a full and conscious breath that begins to shift her experience. Mimi was extremely self-critical when she assumed she had disappointed me by canceling the appointment. The first guiding principle tells her that any identity she holds about herself is made up of distorted and limiting thoughts. Knowing this, she begins to consider that the self-critical thought storm is a conditioned pattern and that the content of these thoughts doesn't accurately describe her. She now has a buffer between her and her thoughts.

The second guiding principle says that believing these thoughts is optional. Even if she believes she disappointed me, this principle suggests that there may be other ways to hold this moment. Bringing openness to the situation, she can consider that maybe I wasn't frustrated with her, maybe she didn't do anything wrong, maybe she can let all the content go and just breathe.

The third guiding principle offers the possibility of having control over shifting her attention to different aspects of her experience. She realizes that she doesn't have to be taken down the road of this familiar thought pattern. What can she do? The fourth guiding principle opens her to being aware in the present moment beyond her thoughts and feelings. What fresh way of being is possible?

Can you feel how these principles challenge the apparent reality of this identity? Can you taste the potential for knowing something beyond it?

Recognizing this reactive tendency and the suffering it brings, Mimi invokes the five core practices:

1.  She turns toward her experience with openness, curiosity, and the desire to know what's false and what's true.

2.  By doing so, she discovers the safe haven of being aware of her thinking pattern and emotions, rather than being gripped by them.

3.  She recognizes the beliefs she holds—that she shouldn't have canceled the appointment, that something is wrong with her if she displeases others—and sees how believing these thoughts brings about suffering. She takes her time with the invitation to lose interest in her thinking. She gradually understands that these beliefs were learned when she was young and that what they say doesn't describe her true essence. She loses interest in the content of these thoughts, as she stays grounded in the spaciousness of being aware.

4.  Bringing her attention to physical sensations, she takes a breath and notices the heaviness of shame and the flush of embarrassment and anxiety. She welcomes these sensations fully with the deepest acceptance.

5.  Experiencing being free of this identity in the moment, she discovers the peace of her true nature. It may be for just a short time, but she begins to realize that suffering is optional.

Self-critical thoughts may start up again quite easily, but each time they come is a moment to meet them with the guiding principles and core practices.

Applying those principles and practices to your experience doesn't mean that an identity will disappear or that painful feelings will dissolve forever. *The only time you're suffering is in the moment, and the only time you can be free of suffering is in the moment.* These deeply conditioned patterns will recur because they've lived in your mind and body for a long time. They have a momentum that takes time to weaken.

Years ago, I was doggedly applying the five practices to every moment of suffering—not to reach a goal, but to be present in those moments with what I was experiencing. One morning I woke up and the thought came to me that I hadn't been sad for months. There was no dramatic moment of change or feeling that I'd accomplished something. There was simply the insight that I was happy.

Refer to your journaling from the last reflection. Take one familiar reaction that developed in your childhood that still brings suffering. Consider it in terms of the four guiding principles:

1. You're veiled by thoughts that are distorted and false.

2. Believing those thoughts is optional.

3. You don't have to be locked into this way of thinking. You can shift your attention to different parts of your experience.

4. You can explore your experience beyond your thoughts and feelings.

And apply the five core practices:

1. Turn toward your experience with openness, curiosity, kindness, and dedication.

2. Meet it from the safe haven of being aware.

3. Lose interest in the content of these limiting thoughts.

4. Welcome feelings and sensations with love and acceptance.

5. The separate identity dissolves as you experience the sacred return to pure awareness. Enjoy your natural self, relaxed, still, and free of conditioning.

# Dynamics in Relationships

When we aren't securely attached in our early relationships with our parents or caregivers, our needs for safety aren't met. Growing up feeling insecure and unlovable, we develop strategies that help us cope. Some of us dissociate from our experience and go through life unable to connect. Some of us put up walls, keeping our relationships brief and superficial. Some of us turn away from the inner sense of lack and glom on to others, looking for their acceptance and approval.

In order to uncover these deeply held conditioned tendencies, we need to explore the habitual patterns in our interpersonal relationships to find the identity that underlies them.

Lois was raised in an extremely turbulent home, with constant chaos and raised voices. She was criticized for just about everything—who she chose as friends, how she kept her room, the food she ate, the opinions she shared. She came out of that environment with a nervous system in perpetual heightened arousal and a tendency to define herself only by others' opinions of her.

As a young woman, she quickly formed relationships with men to ease the emptiness and anxiety she felt inside. But, as many of us do, she ended up with partners who re-created the familiar environment of her childhood, marked by drama and disapproval. With no trust in her own intuitions, she defined herself by others' critical remarks, concluding that she was unworthy of love, incapable as a mother, and unable to cope with the normal ups and downs of life. She could be demanding, judgmental, and angry with others when all she longed for was positive attention and loving support.

When I met Lois, her limited personal identity was strongly intact. When I invited her to consider that she could inquire into the ways she defined herself to see if they were actually true, she responded with a rush of justifications for believing she was unworthy.

Over time, she realized she could trust me as a reliable source of clarity and support. She learned skills to calm her nervous system, which helped her turn toward her own experience rather than always looking to others for support. When she asked me questions about what to do, I suggested that she turn inward to get to know her own inner knowing, which she eventually realized had always been there. Gradually she became more trusting of herself, kinder to others, and more able to exit situations in which she was treated poorly. She was able to breathe through her emotions when she was triggered so she was less stressed, which gave her more time to enjoy friends and family. Her tendency to worry slowly began to subside and her sleep improved. Her fun-loving nature had more space to shine.

What do you bring to the dynamics in your relationships? Do you tend to be pushy, passive, withdrawing, melancholy, anxious, or needy? Do you see other people as threatening or controlling, or as objects to be manipulated? Do you believe that others hold the key to your happiness—if only they would give it to you? Is it hard for you to be relaxed and open? These strategies all have an agenda—to keep yourself safe and get something you think you don't have. They are likely residues from not experiencing secure attachments with adults early on in your life.

These interpersonal strategies are based on how you define yourself, which includes the beliefs you hold to be true and the emotions that underlie them. Do these beliefs about your personal inadequacy make you feel separate? Absolutely. They keep you busy managing your reactions, trying to get your needs met, and distanced from the peace that's here at the heart of any moment. Leaving them unexplored keeps your sense of the separate self very much intact. You can't help but be self-absorbed.

Recognizing these strategies is the first step to finding freedom from them. Once you shine the spotlight on how you're pulled to relate in your interactions with others, you can begin to unwind the underlying beliefs. You recognize what the guiding principles tell you: that self-beliefs that make you suffer are distorted—and optional. And you realize that you don't have to engage with them—you can open awareness to the whole of your experience instead. Then, applying the practices, you take a breath and turn toward your in-the-moment experience—the empty hole of needing to please, the terror of being disapproved of, the intense agitation that takes over your body. Taking your stand as the witnessing presence, you lose interest in thoughts and lovingly welcome your emotions.

This is how suffering serves. You realize you're in the prison of limiting personal beliefs driven by painful emotions, and you change your relationship to your experience. What do you discover? That you're not the one who feels deprived and lacking. You're the space that this identity arises in—luminous, pure, and already free.

Who doesn't get caught in the muck of conditioned tendencies? I know I do. I'll catch myself closing down out of fear or not staying present due to my judging mind. But I also know that each of these moments contains a seed of possibility. Realizing that, you can always turn toward your experience, question it, love it, and find your way to peace beyond the echo of the personal self.

Coming from a place of compassion and clear seeing, let's get curious about what you bring to the dynamics in your relationships, especially when they don't feel harmonious and peaceful. Take your time completing the following statements.

I want people to _____.

When I think of connecting with people, I feel

_____.

I'm most relaxed with people when _____.

I feel most anxious around people when _____.

In relationships, I'm usually _____.

I feel I don't matter when _____.

I get angry at people when _____.

I withdraw from people when _____.

I seek out people when _____.

Find the patterns you play out, and bring them to the guiding principles and core practices, following the examples in this section. Be open to any discoveries that appear.

# When You're Stuck in the Past

If you're living in the content of the stories you tell yourself about the past, you're not looking outside the story to explore the totality of your present-moment experience. You're caught in the details of who did what to whom and what should or shouldn't have happened. Your mind is busy running a commentary filled with opinions and judgments on events that happened long ago and how they affect you now.

Some of these thought patterns are subtle, as we'll see below. If you feel like you're a victim of others' actions, you'll blame them for your suffering—and feel powerless to do anything about it. And if you wish things had been different, your mind is caught in thoughts about the past and you're missing out on the here-and-now opportunity to discover the freedom that's possible. See if these patterns resonate with you.

## Identifying as a Victim

If you think you're a victim of the things that happened, you'll stay lodged in the identity as the one who was wronged. There's no question that we sometimes encounter difficult experiences and that people don't always treat us well. But getting lost in believing you're a victim of others' actions invites the mind to keep justifying these beliefs. And it keeps you endlessly repeating a story with no way out.

Identifying as a victim means that you believe the actions of others have caused your distress. It takes away your power to work with your own experience.

Recognize the victim story you tell yourself, and see how it makes you feel. You'll notice that you feel angry, passive, and resigned. There's a strong sense of the personal "me" in the victim story: "This shouldn't have happened to me. I got born into the wrong family. I'm entitled to an apology." Can you feel the separation in these statements? Not just the separation of you from others, but separation from your in-the-moment authentic experience.

This story is a clever strategy of the mind that protects you from experiencing difficult feelings. It's a way of resisting your experience. If you keep looking outward for resolution, not only will you not find it, you're ignoring the sadness, loss, and anger you probably feel. Meeting these feelings in deep acceptance and love offers the possibility of being free of the pain.

The victim story is an energy vampire. And seeing beyond it brings you to intimacy with your experience. Where before you were avoiding emotions by looking for solutions "out there," now you're open to fully knowing this tender part of your present-moment experience and the peace that lies at the heart of it.

Just as an experiment, play with losing interest in the victim story. Become aware of the thoughts that support it and how you feel when you think these thoughts. Use these inquiry questions from chapter 5:

    ⚛   What is this thought? How did it appear? What is it exactly? (Remember that a thought is made up of sounds that you've learned have a certain meaning.)

- ❧ Do I need this thought? Is it essential?

- ❧ Does it serve me or anyone else? Is it helpful or useful?

- ❧ Is the content of this thought agitating, neutral, or relaxing?

- ❧ Can I lose interest in the content of this thought?

Now are you ready to meet the feelings you've been avoiding? With great compassion, turn toward your feelings. Be the welcoming space that allows them all to come to the light of conscious awareness. Giving up the victim story paves the way for resolution, space, and peace.

## Blame and Resentment

If you catch yourself blaming others, you'll keep the story of you as a victim intact. You'll feel that you lack what you think you need to resolve the past.

You may have convinced yourself that others are responsible for the suffering you experience, and the urge to blame may be very strong. Blaming consists of a constellation of thoughts and physical tensions in the body. These experiences may be highly conditioned in you, making it challenging to see things any other way. Unwinding this long-held story and the effects of it may take time, and you might benefit from sessions with a professional counselor. So don't hesitate to seek help.

But know this: blame and resentment will keep you resisting—and suffering. It will keep you from getting curious about your present-moment experience. Turning toward these thoughts and feelings offers you the beautiful opportunity to awaken to the truth of being free of stories.

Following the core practices, lose interest in the content of blaming thoughts, recognizing that they don't serve your peace and happiness. You'll notice emotions living in your body asking for the loving attention they need for their liberation. From the safe haven of being aware, welcome the energies and sensations without creating a story around them. It's the most loving way to be with your experience.

This is a tender process that chips away at the old identities you developed from challenging past experiences. Eventually, opening to your personal pain opens you to the universal pain of the human condition. Everyone on earth who believes their own thoughts suffers to some degree. By meeting your own pain with compassion, you may notice a newfound capacity to understand the behavior of others.

If some people hurt you when you were young, remember that they were driven by unexamined belief systems and emotions lying outside of conscious awareness. They may have felt overwhelmed, entitled, out of control, or fearful. Maybe they were embarrassed, frustrated, or self-absorbed. Perhaps a pattern laid down for generations in their family was being expressed without them being aware of it.

Getting perspective on the context behind someone else's misguided behavior doesn't make the behavior acceptable, but it does soften the urge to blame. This is the reality: tough things happen in life. Without investigating our reactions to these circumstances, we view them through the eyes of separation that reinforce the feeling of being wounded and victimized, and we harshly judge the other. But there's another way, which is to use all our reactions as opportunities for awakening from the trance of our limited belief systems. The personal story falls away, and we're left with hearts full of love and understanding.

If you blame others as the cause of your suffering, consider that this viewpoint leaves you believing you lack what you need to be at peace.

What if you instead turned your loving attention to embrace your own experience? With openness in your mind and body, bring your experience to the four guiding principles and five core practices (see appendix). What insights do you realize? How do you see things differently from the perspective of awakened awareness? What remains in you that is asking for loving attention?

## Wishful Thinking

Many of us hold the belief that if only the past had been different, we would be more content in our current lives. Of course, we all want to be happy. But this "if only" mind-set is a kind of fantasy. It's wishful thinking about what might have been and doesn't meet the truth as it is.

What's amazing is that the happiness you seek is possible, but it won't come from wishing, hoping, or waiting. These are mind traps that keep you from opening to your present-moment experience. When your mind holds a vision of how you wished things were or how you want them to be in the future, you're ignoring what's happening now.

If you wish you had had different parents, if you're hoping you'll feel better at some point in the future, or if you're waiting for an apology that you think will make things right for you, then your attention is grabbed by a thought pattern about the past or future and diverted from knowing the peace that's possible right now.

Resisting what is true is a defining feature of the separate self, and opening to the reality of things is the way through. You can't change the past, but you *can* shift how you relate to the reactions that appear now. You might experience more pain as you open to the feelings that have been suppressed for so long. But it takes a lot of energy to defend against them, and doing so keeps you living in stories that separate you from peace.

Reflecting on your perspective on what happened to you in the past, are you caught in wishful thinking? Are you waiting or hoping for things to improve?

Journal on the following questions:

1.  What do you get out of wishing the past had been different?

2.  Seeing what happened clearly and not through your hopes and dreams, what do you notice?

3.  What are you experiencing now that you avoid by hoping for a better past or future?

Now be with your in-the-moment experience with the support of the guiding principles and core practices.

## Do You Need to Forgive?

I like to do crossword puzzles, and one day I came across the clue for a six-letter word meaning "something you hold or nurse." The answer? Grudge.

This clue offers a recipe for how to keep a grudge—you hold on tight, feeding it with your attention so it stays lodged in your mind. And what are you cherishing so dearly? As the dictionary defines it, "a feeling of ill will or resentment."

If you focus on the terrible things someone did to you, even though the actual behavior stopped long ago, who's being hurt? You're still hurting yourself in your mind.

Forgiveness has little to do with anyone else; it is an inner shift that happens when you turn your attention to your own experience with openness and curiosity. You stop spinning in the story of the events and the beliefs about what should and shouldn't have happened. And you lovingly meet the pain—going right to the physical sensations inhabiting your body and accepting them deeply. That's what you can do in your own quiet moments to free yourself from the past.

When you bring the guiding principles to the grudge you hold, you see that the thoughts are distorted, that believing them is optional, and that focusing on them keeps you from experiencing freedom. With the intention to be free, you bring your attention to your identity as the one who was wronged. Seeing it with clarity, it's a constellation of misleading thoughts and painful feelings that make you feel separate. In the spaciousness of being aware, all is welcomed in the timeless now.

These stories of being wronged hold on tightly, and moving past them can take time. Whenever they appear and you feel caught, don't feed them with your attention. Instead, do something to shift your experience:

| | | |
|---|---|---|
| ❧ Stop | | ❧ Welcome |
| ❧ Open | | ❧ Befriend |
| ❧ Breathe | | ❧ Accept |
| ❧ Notice | | ❧ Embrace |
| ❧ Explore | | ❧ Be |

# The Sacred Return

The direct path to knowing yourself as consciousness awake to itself has no steps and no practices. In the moments when attention is fully released from the contents of the mind, you leave the realm of time and space and the sense of the separate self vanishes into infinite, timeless knowing of pure awareness. This is the sacred return.

Emerging back into the world of form with this understanding, you see everything through the truth that separation isn't real. Whatever thoughts and feelings arise, you know in your heart of hearts that it's impossible for anything to be lacking or missing. You're prone to enthusiasm, joy, and appreciation, and you hold everything lightly.

If the veil of separation falls away easily, take the direct path to knowing your true nature, over and over. Abandon the attachment to any objects, and live from formless being. But if your conditioned mind is firmly in place, loosen its grip by working your way through the guiding principles and core practices.

No matter what is happening—whether you're caught or free—life continually unfolds, completely undisturbed by your thoughts about it. Know yourself as already in harmony with this unfolding.

# Summary

For most of us, the roots of our identity as broken or inadequate are found in the way we think about our past experiences. This chapter has offered several areas for contemplation that encourage having a friendly relationship with our past.

What happened in the past isn't the problem—what needs attention is how we hold the past now. We looked at how ruptures in trust in our early relationships can lead to the belief that we're unworthy. As children, when we don't get what we need, we assume it's because there's something wrong with us. And we don't learn the skills to intelligently handle our emotions.

Feelings hide outside of awareness, and we scramble to find our grounding in the confusion of the mind. The guiding principles and core practices invite our loving attention to our experience of suffering in the moments when it arises, and they offer a pathway to resolution and clear seeing.

This chapter also brought attention to:

- ✵ Dynamics we bring to our relationships that are based on early ruptures in trust;

- ✵ Ways we resist opening to our present-moment experience—identifying as a victim, blaming others, and wishful thinking; and

- ✵ Holding a grudge, and the need to forgive.

No matter how we hold on to resentments about the past, freedom from them is always possible. In any moment, we can apply the guiding principles and core practices.

And here we are, unveiled, free of the prison of separation, openhearted and fully alive.

In the next chapter we'll look at another painful way we feel separate—taking things personally. Who is the one who is able to be hurt by the actions of others? Let's clear up this confusion and discover essential peace and happiness.

# CHAPTER 9

# THE PAIN OF TAKING THINGS PERSONALLY

Before pain was, you were.
After pain had gone, you remained.
Pain is transient, you are not.

—Nisargadatta Maharaj

Marsha grew up in a family with incredibly high standards of perfection kept in place with rampant criticism. Anything that happened that was the least bit out of the ordinary was met with an explosion of drama about who was at fault. She was constantly on guard, waiting for the next judgment to be thrown her way.

At some point in her twenties, Marsha was flying in to meet her family for a weekend gathering and her sister was picking her up at the airport. She was anxiously sitting toward the back of the plane, which arrived an hour late, already feeling responsible for making her sister wait. Then the flight attendants requested that all passengers with connecting flights exit the plane first. Being the last one to walk off the plane, she was terrified of the onslaught of criticism she was about to receive from her sister.

Can you feel Marsha's pain? She felt responsible for her lateness even though the reasons were completely out of her control.

You take things personally when you view the world through the veil of your own inadequacy—and it hurts. Taking things personally means that you define who you are by sources outside yourself—the words and actions of other people. Someone says or does something, and you assume that it means something negative about yourself— that you're bad, wrong, unworthy, unlovable, incapable, or broken. You're a magnet for feeling responsible for everyone else's suffering. If things aren't perfect, then you must be the one who's at fault. If a man is late for a date with you, you conclude that you must not be worthy of his respect. If someone doesn't call, she must be thinking of all the reasons why she wants to reject your friendship.

My client Joan is highly conditioned to compare herself to others and come up lacking. A coworker made a remark about a positive quality of another person on their team. Even though he said nothing about her one way or the other, she immediately felt put down because she received no such compliment.

See how the thinking mind is so powerful! It quickly distorts the truth of things and we feel a stab of emotional pain. And if this pain goes unnoticed and isn't met in the loving space of being aware, the mind starts running with its sad and self-critical stories. Before you know it, you're lost again in the identity of not being good enough. Untethered and floating in a sea of negative thoughts and hurt feelings, you've overlooked the possibility of turning inward toward your in-the-moment experience. You've forgotten the essence of who you are beyond all thoughts.

In this chapter we'll break down the experience of taking things personally so you can recognize when it happens. We'll go through ways to work with your thoughts and feelings to come to the understanding that others' words and actions are not about you. Throughout, I invite you over and over to question what you take to be real and to turn toward yourself with kindness, acceptance, and love. You *can* find your way through to discover the peace untouched by thoughts of lack and inadequacy.

## The Prison of Personal Suffering

The impact of taking things personally is far-reaching, in the ways I will address below. These problems come from identifying as the separate, thought-based self and forgetting your true identity as the aliveness at the heart of everything. Understand how you get caught in suffering, and you're on the path to discovering the peace of your true nature.

### Self-Betrayal

When I first heard the term "self-betrayal" and understood what it meant, it hit me like a lightning bolt. I realized that every time I moved away from myself and into the distorted content of my thoughts, I was betraying myself. Acting as if I actually was the inadequate and unworthy one defined by my limiting story, I was afraid of living the truth of my essential limitlessness. I was afraid of not knowing what to do, afraid of being rejected if I stood in that truth, and afraid of the backlash from not meeting others' expectations of me.

When we betray ourselves, we set ourselves up to be a sponge for others' reactions to us. We define ourselves by things the people around us say and do. *We've given up the power of the truth about who we are to an unreliable and confused source of information.*

The term "self-betrayal" inspired me to be fearless, and maybe it will do the same for you. I stopped scanning the environment and turned within. I stopped immediately thinking I was wrong or damaged whenever anything happened.

If you personalize things that happen around you without realizing you're doing so, you will be betraying yourself. You're believing that what others say and do is about you, and you're ignoring the truth of who you are. You're worshipping at the altar of old belief systems. What's amazing? To know that you can return to yourself in any moment.

---

Now it's your turn to contemplate self-betrayal. Before you get out your journal, take a moment to close your eyes and find compassion and acceptance within. Then write at the top of a page "How do I betray myself?" and write continuously for at least three minutes.

Then write about this question: What situations trigger self-betrayal?

Sit quietly and reflect on what you've discovered. What would it be like to trust yourself?

---

## How Relationships Are Affected

It's impossible to take things personally and not have your relationships limited in some important way. When you feel the "Ouch!" of hurt feelings, here's what can happen:

- You go inward to lick your wounds and suffer silently as you try to show a brave face to the world.

- You feel threatened and react by distancing yourself from others or judging them in your thoughts.

- You'll do anything to please others, even at your own expense.

- You're afraid to set necessary boundaries that you fear will threaten your connections.

- You expect to be abandoned or mistreated, and life complies with these expectations.

If you play out any of these examples, you're living the experience of separation.

Andrea and her husband were locked in a dance that was exhausting both of them. She constantly expressed her emotional needs and felt angry when he couldn't meet them perfectly. He took it on himself to be the one to fix all her flaws. Together more than twenty years, they moved among passion, distance, and conflict, with little space for the loving relationship they both wanted.

As you can see, the dynamics in our relationships don't happen in isolation. Both people contribute to how the interactions unfold. But this dance can change in any moment. Be willing to look at your contribution as you become an expert in the dynamics you play out. What propels you to forget yourself and please others, or to hide behind a wall of fear?

With great kindness toward yourself, discover the subtle conditioned patterns that may have become so familiar to you that it's hard to see outside them. Know what you have come to believe that isn't true. Only then are you free to experiment with new ways of being in relationships that are authentic and true.

Take some time to reflect:

- How do you protect yourself from being rejected or abandoned?

- How do you relate to others when you feel wounded by their actions?

Bring each of these expressions of the separate self to the guiding principles and core practices. Putting these tendencies aside, brainstorm fresh ways you might show up in your relationships.

## How Others Treat You

There is much written in the pop psychology literature about boundaries. If you take things personally and need to please others to try to fill yourself up, you may not be setting healthy boundaries. You may find that others take advantage of you or treat you poorly. This happens when you're so lost in beliefs that tell you you're unworthy that you become a target for their demands.

The good news, as you know by now, is that this identity of unworthiness does not accurately reflect who you are. When you see through this limited way of being, the need to please others dissolves and you're available to set limits the situation calls for. You step off the hamster wheel of your conditioned reaction to always say yes to others' demands and requests. You're now free to ask yourself: What is the best course of action? What is the situation actually calling for?

Take the drivers of fear and lack out of the equation, and you're open to being moved by the truth of the moment—which is far more intelligent than your personal needs and desires.

My client Gina had given her adult son tens of thousands of dollars to help him with living expenses when he relapsed into his drug addiction. He hadn't paid any of it back, despite her requests. As I listened to her talk about her concerns, I was thinking that there was no way she was ever going to see this money. Her whole demeanor felt weak. She spoke softly in a questioning tone, as if she didn't deserve to be repaid, and she was obviously fearful of upsetting her son.

Gina was courageous about opening to the fear and unworthiness she experienced. She was very ready for this work, excited to try out new ways of being. Turning toward her experience, she discovered a host of reactions she hadn't been aware of. She opened to the fear of displeasing her son, but even deeper was a long-standing hidden feeling that she didn't deserve to express her needs or to have them be met.

Welcoming these feelings fully in the light of awareness, she told me that it felt like even the cells of her body were rearranging. We role-played some scenarios so she could practice requesting the money without her familiar fears, and she went out and had these conversations with her son. Her worst fear, that he would reject her, never materialized. He didn't immediately repay her, but she felt a tremendous sense of inner power by discovering she didn't have to define herself by feelings of unworthiness.

What Gina experienced was a crack in the solid identity that let in the light of new possibilities. The power of present-moment awareness now had the space to move through her. And it moved her to handle situations with intelligence and grace. Her mind had less to ruminate on, and she began to experience many moments of peace.

Each of these moments is a cause for celebration.

Be open and courageous as you tiptoe into freedom, beyond any limiting thoughts about yourself. Lovingly meet your fears of rejection, and stand in the space of truth. It's a powerful place to be! Without the need to please or protect, where does that leave you? Experiment with taking the necessary actions that come from clarity and wishing well-being for all, including yourself.

---

Picture in your mind someone who triggers your feelings of inadequacy. See yourself standing in front of this person.

- How do you feel in your body as you're facing him or her?

- What do you feel moved to do or say?

- Imagine putting aside any conditioned tendencies that define you. Now how do you feel in your body without them? Stand up and feel the bold power of truth.

∽ What do you feel moved to do or say that may be new for you?

Repeat this inquiry for any other people in your life who make it hard for you to set clear boundaries.

Let yourself get used to this new expansiveness and the possibilities it brings. Only when you're ready, you may want to experiment with interacting in these new ways.

Others may not be pleased when you stop the old relationship dance and show up in truth. Keep breathing, and stay aware and grounded in yourself. Navigate the situation as best you can. It may take time for others to adapt to your new ways of being.

## Muting Your Zest for Life

If you take things personally, you've convinced yourself that how you think others perceive you is true. You believe that you're actually worthy of rejection and that you don't matter. The result? You lose the natural zest for living that comes with the freedom of knowing the truth of who you are, undefined by any stories. You deny yourself the opportunity to flourish in your talents and passions, and you talk yourself out of success before you even get started. These effects are far-reaching and painful.

For some of us, this is what we might call the ordinary suffering of daily life. We're so used to living under the spell of these limiting self-beliefs that we don't consider that another way to relate to our experience is possible. And we lose touch with the true knowing of who we are—and who we're not.

It's draining to live with the eyes of the hungry ghost, looking for the love and attention that you think will complete you and feeling like you're always missing the mark. There's little space for your natural inclinations to emerge, and if they do, you put up roadblocks that sabotage your accomplishments. You're actually playing a role, like an actor in a movie, but you believe the script is real.

The hurt that comes from taking things personally is optional. While we're occupied with feeling badly about ourselves, blaming others, and striving to find what we think we're missing, what we're really missing out on is the life that's unfolding right here and now. And it is overflowing with possibility.

The reality of the moment is so incredibly full. Just look around you. Even if you're in a prison or in a high-rise building with no view, even if your only apparent reality is the prison of your own negative thinking, everything is teeming with life. Just notice your breath and feel the life that can't help but animate your body. How do you discover this fullness? You stop listening to others' views of you and the contents of your sadness-inducing thoughts. You recognize your limiting conditioned patterns and put them aside so that you're available to step fully into the life that's being offered you—right now.

Here are more questions for contemplation or journaling:

- How has taking things personally affected your life? What impact has it had on your relationships? Your career? The way you spend your time? Any other effects?

- If you didn't believe the conclusions you've drawn about yourself and you returned to your natural innocence, what would you do? How would you express yourself in the world? What are you enthusiastic about? Let yourself be surprised by what you discover.

# The Promise: Not Taking Things Personally

There is so much freedom that comes from not taking things personally. The world can swirl around you, people can insult you or criticize you or express other hostile opinions, but you're immune to the effects. And you're free to take in any feed back you receive without it crushing you.

This doesn't mean that you don't react emotionally. The brain and nervous system are programmed to fire if they perceive danger. But when an emotion occurs, you don't resist it, and you attend to the sensations in your body by holding them like a loving mother holds her child.

What becomes immune to the events of the outside world is not your illusory separate self. The beliefs that you're unworthy and lacking don't get fixed. You don't change these statements into better ones and then believe them. And you don't miraculously discover that this self you thought was broken was actually whole all along.

The freedom comes when you realize that this separate self is only a constellation of thoughts and feelings and that these are objects that arise within the truth of you, which is awakened presence. When you know in your bones that the beliefs that make up your separate self are false, you're then inspired to look elsewhere to know what is real about you.

And where do you look? You bring your attention directly to your own experience. Not looking to others or to your thoughts for self-definition, you discover that without these, something in you is still very much alive. Then you realize that this aliveness is all-encompassing. The sense of separation falls away, and you endlessly expand into consciousness as the source of everything.

From here, how could you possibly take things personally? There's nowhere for anything to stick or land.

The simple solution to the problem of taking things personally is to stop doing it. If you can do that, you can celebrate the grace of the direct path. This means that awakened awareness is alive in your conscious experience. You might still notice old habits—the beliefs that you now know aren't true and the emotions that you experience as only physical sensation without the story—but your primary experience is an uncluttered mind and deep relaxation. You're open to all that is in the formless, timeless space from which all of life flows.

If the direct path isn't available to you right now, don't worry. You've been given the tools you need to deconstruct the tendencies that run in you, and they will help you. Pull these tendencies apart bit by bit until they don't have the power to deceive you any longer.

You can embody the guiding principles to remind you of the nature of conditioned habits and the possibility of the pure knowing of experience free of conditioning. And you can walk through the five core practices so you're available to the sacred return back to yourself—not the personal self that lacks and needs, but the truth of you that is open and untouched.

> Think back on your responses to the reflections you did earlier in this chapter. Choose one or two ways that you take things personally. Bring to that identity the four guiding principles and five core practices (see appendix).
>
> Take your time and keep this process real. Experience it not in your mind, but fully alive in all of your being.

## How to Not Take Things Personally

How do you not take things personally? The short answer to this question is to see through your false identification as the limited one who feels hurt, and thus to know the truth of your experience—that there is just the coming and going of objects appearing in the friendly and welcoming space of being aware. And you'll be well on the path to this realization by following the guiding principles and core practices.

When you're gripped by the identity of taking things personally, you might also experiment with the additional tools and insights below to see if they help. These can support you to untie the identification with the separate hurting self. I encourage you to use whatever means are necessary so that, little by little, you will experience the freedom of flowing in harmony with life.

## Know What You Can and Can't Control

When the identity of unworthiness has been triggered and you're lost in the stab of personal pain, contemplate what you can and can't control.

The list of what we can't control is very long. We can't control what other people say or do. We can't control being criticized or abandoned. We can't control someone's defensiveness or lack of response or unwillingness to listen. We have no control over anything to do with "others."

We can't even control the appearance of our own thoughts and feelings.

But there is one thing that we can control, and it's a game changer. What we can control is where we place our attention. Here's what's possible:

- We can stop trying to fix what we can't do anything about.

- We can stop listening to the stories in our minds.

- We can open to meet our own pain from the space of loving awareness.

- And once that tangle of thoughts and feelings subsides, we can discover the peaceful space of presence.

What happens in the outside world is not about you, and you can't do anything about it anyway. When you focus on wanting events and people to be different, you'll stay stuck in longing and pain. But take the wisdom-based path toward your inner experience and get curious about your own reactions. Relate to your inner experience in a new way. You'll find your way through the trance of separation to discover the truth of who you are.

Now you're aligning your efforts with behaviors that will actually relieve your suffering.

Once you stop trying to control what's not controllable, consciousness expands beyond the personal self. Unclogged by the thinking mind, there's space for insight into what's behind someone else's distress, realizing that what they do and say is not about you. You realize that your own thoughts aren't true and you feel great compassion for the part of you that feels personally hurt.

Now that you are free, who knows what will happen? You might connect more deeply with someone or politely withdraw. You might draw a line in the sand about what is and isn't okay with you. You might follow the call to make a significant change in your life. Whatever you do comes from your essential wholeness.

This is the peace—and the power—of awakened awareness.

Use this journaling exercise to reflect on what you can and can't control. Write at least a page on this question: What have I been doing to try to fix the hurt that I feel? Write freely without stopping to think as you go.

Look back on what you've written. Which actions are focused on things you can't control? On things you can control?

From a place of clear seeing and intelligence, make a list of at least five things you *can* do to move through hurt feelings.

These support you to shed the self-identities that diminish your happiness, leaving space for the simple joy of fully living now.

## *Untangle the Story*

I once spoke with Janice, who was still grieving the loss of her mother from forty-five years ago. During our meeting she cried as if her mother had died yesterday. Janice felt responsible for her mother's death, thinking she should have been more attentive to her mother's suffering.

As we unraveled her family history, we were able to pinpoint Janice's misunderstandings and illogical conclusions. She came from a loving family, but one in which no one shared feelings or talked openly when things weren't going well. There was no way she could have known that her mother's health was starting to decline. In addition, her mother died when Janice was twenty-five and just starting a career as a teacher. She was very engaged with this new career, excited about helping others and doing the job well—all normal interests at that stage of life. This career path was seen as a huge success in the family, and her mother was extremely proud of her.

By untangling the story, Janice was able to recognize how important it was that her mother died knowing that Janice was succeeding in life. Once Janice put the pieces together that explained what was happening at the time, she was able to stop feeling that she should have done more for her mother. Freeing up this long-held guilt felt like letting go of a heavy weight she had been carrying around for decades.

Spend some time reflecting on these questions. Look at the facts of the stories you hold on to from your past that make you feel personally wounded or at fault.

- ❧ What facts have you ignored?

- ❧ What interpretations are you living with that aren't true? Consider that you may have misinterpreted others' actions. Go to the facts instead.

- ❧ Look at the situation from different points of view.

If you're having trouble seeing things objectively, don't hesitate to ask a trusted friend to help you, or consult with a counselor in your local area.

## Uncover Hidden Beliefs

You may be holding on to beliefs that set you up to take things personally without realizing it. This was the case for Trudy. She sat in my office overcome by emotions following a breakup. She felt hurt, disappointed, lost, abandoned, and all the other feelings you might expect. And then, in the middle of all this pain, came the golden insight: "The only way out of this pain is to let go."

Before letting go, she needed to identify how she was holding on. This insight prompted an interesting line of inquiry:

- 🌀 What was she holding on to?

- 🌀 What endings did she not want to face?

- 🌀 What was she hoping for that wasn't happening?

🔅 What expectations were hidden below the surface of her awareness?

The answers to these questions revealed so many ways that her attention was stuck in wanting things to be different than they were. She believed her ex should be friendlier. She believed she should still be a part of their social group. She believed his family should want to stay connected to her. Each belief kept her desperately longing for something she felt she was missing and personally offended that she wasn't getting it. It was a big aha moment to realize these expectations—no wonder she was hurting so much!

Together, we went through each belief she discovered and asked: "Can I let go of this?" In her mind, she fleshed out the picture of holding on and what that looked like for everyone involved. Then she pictured how things would look and feel if she let go. The hurt feelings weren't totally gone, but she realized that each time she could say yes to letting go she could fully step into the life that was actually happening and give up the one based on the past that still occupied her thoughts.

In fact, she felt the relief of finally being aligned with the truth of how things are. She felt light, open, expanded, and more peaceful than she thought was possible.

If you want to stop taking things personally, slow down and check to see if you find some underlying beliefs hiding out. In your view, what should or shouldn't be happening? Do you believe any of the following?

🔅 People shouldn't say mean things or criticize.

🔅 They shouldn't leave.

🔅 They shouldn't lie.

🔅 They should want to include you.

🔅 They should always be respectful.

- They should want to listen to everything you have to say.

- They shouldn't break up by a text message.

- Life should be fair.

If you hold these beliefs close without knowing it, you will somehow take it personally when reality doesn't conform to them. But when you become aware of them, you're on your way to discovering that this suffering is optional.

> Think of a situation that troubles you, and find the beliefs at the core of your suffering. Picture the scene in your mind of what it's like to hold on to each belief, and feel the effects in your body. Then picture and feel how things would be for you if you let go.
>
> Notice that I'm not asking you to let go. Just feel into the possibility of not having this belief affect you. Then when you're ready, when grace shines on you, you'll leave the limited world of hopes and expectations and awaken into the timeless reality where there's no place for anything personal to land.

## Navigate with Care in Relationships

Living nonduality means that we're aware of the personal hooks that make us feel fearful and separate from others. We explore them and meet them within, rather than taking them as true. We're living in the unconditioned, moved by love.

This sounds great until we're in relationships and things quickly get muddled. This is the relative reality of the world of form, which seems very real to us, even as we wish to enjoy harmonious connections with others. We get hurt, we hurt others, we fall, we get up, we reconnect and repair, we leave, we stay. This is the nature of human relationships. So how to approach them with openness? How do we stay true to the core knowing of infinite awareness in the face of our own reactions?

There are no simple answers to these questions. But the basic things to start with are to slow down, to stay in touch with yourself, and to navigate with care.

There is much I could say about relationships that is beyond the scope of this book. So here's the important takeaway. In the service of the desire to stay true, cultivate the skill of deep listening. With an open mind, empty of opinions and expectations, and from a place of not knowing any answers, you listen. Listen deeply within—to the whisper of truth and the quiet intelligence that comes through your body. Learn to pay attention to your gut feelings, not to your mind, and have the faith and trust to honor those feelings.

And listen deeply and with openness to others. Rather than getting stuck in same old, same old, show up fresh, with enthusiasm, wonder, and surprise. Do this by wiping the slate clean of history and listening to what arises in the moment.

Where before other people were sources of lack and need, now you're here with them, innocent and curious, needing nothing. Who knows what will happen next?

The true nature of reality is nondual awareness. No one can ever be separate from this truth. Everyone you see is you—not you as a separate self, but you as you truly are, transparent and empty of form. From this understanding emerges a pervasive feeling of good will and benevolence. When we step out of the prison of our own personal suffering, we can see that everyone suffers. At the core, everyone wants to experience joy and happiness.

People are our enemies or threats only when we experience ourselves as separate. In the moments when you see the world through the eyes of the whole, your personal distress dissolves. You'll still react when you're triggered, and you'll want to find your way through places of friction in your relationships. But whatever happens comes from openness, not fear.

> Here is something for you to experiment with that I do often. Go to a public place, such as a café or mall. Sit for a few moments, finding the space of pure being beyond your personal self. Be empty and transparent. Look around you and take in each person as an expression of the one consciousness. Let your heart open endlessly to everyone.
>
> Then bring this same openness and insight to your close relationships.

## Summary

We learned in this chapter that if you identify yourself by the beliefs that you're inadequate or lacking, you are a magnet for suffering. Things happen around you that have little or nothing to do with you, but you interpret them to mean something negative about who you are—you take them personally.

The medicine for these distorted beliefs about yourself is to turn away from absorbing input from others, or even from your own thoughts, and to turn toward your direct experience. Then the guiding principles will reset your perspective and the core practices will invite you into the sacred return to the peace of your true nature.

Taking things personally is painful. We live in stories about ourselves and others while betraying the inner knowing that beyond our stories, we're already whole. We get into unsatisfying relationship dynamics, and while our attention is occupied tending to our pain, we're missing out on fully living the life that's here right now.

Not taking things personally leaves us open to life. We feel others' pain and confusion without drawing negative conclusions about ourselves.

To not take things personally, it helps to be clear about what we can and can't control, to untangle the story by viewing it objectively, to uncover hidden beliefs that create resistance, and to navigate relationships from the knowing of nonseparate reality. These perspectives clear the fog that comes from believing the narrative of the separate self. Then you can bring your attention away from the outer world and into your own experience. You lose interest in distorted thoughts, welcome emotions with loving acceptance, and, as the sense of separation starts to collapse, experience the sacred return back to the timeless now.

In our final chapter we continue the conversation of living an embodied life informed by the teachings of nonduality. If the human body is primed for fear, and the world is full of people living from limited identities, how do we live from love and openness? It's a practical question with implications for everyday life. Let's find out…

# CHAPTER 10

# LIVING THE AWAKENED LIFE

Let your way be the way of water:
If you want to be at peace,
Flow with the stream.

—Lao-tzu

Julie had a difficult go of it when she was young, growing up in a chaotic home with a controlling, demanding mother. Julie was perceptive about what was going on in her home, but for years her mother shamed her for the feelings she experienced and told her that her view of things was wrong. Fast forward to her forties, and Julie had no trust in her own perceptions. Highly traumatized, she would shake with fear when she thought she might have said or done something that displeased someone else, and she absorbed others' criticisms like a sponge.

Our work together was a beautiful unfolding into discovering the stable inner ground of knowing that she realized she could trust. It took a while, but little by little she learned to calm her nervous system so she could see things more clearly and bring her attention away from others' input and into the expansiveness of unconditioned space. Each time she was agitated, she started with a full and conscious breath, then reminded herself that the judgments in her mind weren't true. As she lost interest in thoughts and the bodily feeling of stress subsided, she began navigating situations with a clearer mind. As the veils of separation dropped, she could stay stable in the face of criticism. She parented more effectively, set limits with difficult people in her life, and made decisions that included her own well-being. She felt so much better. It was an honor to watch her transformation.

This way of being in the world is absolutely possible for you, too. If the tendency to think of yourself as inadequate and broken has been your constant companion, step by step, moment by moment, you can turn toward your experience with great kindness and work with it by applying the guiding principles and core practices.

You may stumble along at first, not knowing what to do. You'll get caught again countless times because that's the nature of conditioning. But here is what I know to be true: your true nature is peace itself. You'll discover that you don't *have to* live in limitation and the suffering it brings. Keep returning your attention to the safe haven of being aware, and from here the personal identities will lose their grip. You'll realize that suffering is optional.

## Befriending Fear

The belief in personal inadequacy is rooted in fear, and this fear keeps us from experiencing the effortless openness of our true nature. These fears seem to have no end. You're afraid of failure, of success, of doing it wrong, of judgment, of abandonment, of being exposed as an imposter. Your mind has convinced you that you just can't relax and be natural and free.

So it serves you to get to know fear well. If fear is deeply hidden or vibrating just below the surface of awareness, you'll feel the painful effects of it without knowing what to do. But when you recognize fear, immediately your relationship to it shifts. You can feel it, question it, and deflate its power so you can get back to the business of enjoying life.

Fear: it's a word, a set of letters that we agree has a certain meaning, and it's a label for physical agitation in your body and a distorted pattern of thinking in the mind. Let's learn more about it.

## The Fear Body

The body's fear response begins in the brain. As we learned earlier, our brains are wired to perceive danger so that the body can get into gear and take the actions needed to ensure its survival. Your senses perceive what is happening in the world—they see, hear, taste, touch, and smell. If something is perceived that sets off alarm bells indicating danger, a message travels to the brain structure called the hypothalamus, which sends the nervous system into "fight or flight" mode.

This overactive nervous system is probably well known to you. Think of how you would feel if you suddenly came across a shadowy figure in a dark alley. Your heart rate increases, muscles tense, the stomach churns, and you're highly alert and ready to act.

When you live under the spell of believing you're unworthy, you experience a chronic state of this physical overreactivity. You might not always feel that sudden burst of nervous system activation, but there is a constant low level of stress and muscle tension that has become your reality. Maybe you feel it in your temples, jaw, throat, or chest. It's what we often call anxiety or stress, the hum of the body reacting as if it's threatened, even when the threat is only imagined in your mind. These physical contractions are asking for your attention because they are at the heart of the sense of separation.

You can ignore the physical sensations related to fear or anxiety, or you can recognize them when they appear. You do that by shifting attention to the open space of being aware and welcoming the sensations. Immediately you're less engaged with what these sensations mean—they're seen as just an experience that happens to be arising in the moment. You bring a relaxed presence to them that softens their impact and expands your focus.

The breath is a support as you turn toward the sensations of fear. When you feel anxious or afraid, taking a conscious breath is the knock on the door that helps you lose interest in the mind and opens you to your inner experience. A slow inhale and longer exhale invites physical calm and relaxation and is a message to the nervous system that all is well.

I've spent countless hours sitting quietly as the welcoming presence for the sensations of fear and anxiety. When I first became curious about how I suffered, every time I felt sensations of fear I would sit down on my couch, open into the being-aware space, and welcome them. There were so many sensations I had never noticed before! Something felt absolutely right about this practice.

Sometimes the sensations dissipate and sometimes they don't. In the end it doesn't matter because whenever they arise, you meet them in openness. Doing this practice, you're staying open to life in the form that's being offered to you in the moment—with no goal or expectation in mind.

Experiment with this practice when you feel afraid, tense, or anxious. Sit quietly and take three to five slow, conscious breaths. Inhale and exhale in a rhythm that feels natural to you.

Return to normal breathing, and shift to being the still and silent awareness. From here, you are now knowingly aligned with the welcoming presence that allows all physical sensations just to be.

Since there's no goal to achieve, there's no defined end point to this practice. Stay with it for as long as it feels right, then move on to the next thing. Any time you're feeling anxious, · you can breathe and open to whatever sensations are present.

## The Fear Mind

The voice of fear that runs in your mind is designed to protect you from danger. The truth is that we never know what's going to happen, but the brain on fear is terrified of the unknown. If it doesn't know, it can't protect you, so what does it do? It hijacks your logical mind and spins endless scary stories about the negative events that might happen in the future. If you believe these stories, you'll be prepared to react to this imagined danger.

Does your inner critic torment you? Does it tell you what you can't do and won't accomplish? This is the voice of fear protecting you from failure. Are you highly vigilant about others' reactions, living in fear of the rejection you just know will happen? This is fear's way of helping you avoid pain.

Occasionally, fear is helpful. The physical reaction of fear in the body and the thoughts that come with it signal you to take notice of situations going on around you. When I realize I'm feeling fear, I briefly check in to see if something needs my attention. If action is needed, I take it. But most of the time, it's just the remnant of an old conditioned reaction, so I turn away from the thoughts, feel the sensations, then move on.

The fearful mind is made up of thoughts designed to project every negative outcome imaginable. Believing these ideas makes us suffer. That's why we need to learn to spot when these fear-based thoughts take hold.

## Worry

Worry is one of the ways fear speaks. It tries to get a sense of control over the unknowable and uncontrollable future. Worry produces a rush of anxious questions: What if I don't know what to do? What if something bad happens? How will I deal with it? What should I do? What is she going to say?

I remember standing in the courtyard of a yoga studio waiting for a workshop to begin. I struck up a conversation with a woman who let out a stream of questions: "How many people are coming? What will the teacher be like? How long will the lunch break be?" My answer to all of these questions was: "I don't know." I felt so much compassion for the suffering the fear of the unknown was bringing her.

When you worry about the future, you've lost trust in the unfolding of life. Realizing that you truly can't know what will happen, you acknowledge the want-to-know mind by turning away from it. Then you're prepared to stand in the ground of pure being and trust what comes, meeting each moment with openness. Can you feel how different that is from worrying? Life stops feeling like a constant threat as you align with its unfolding right now.

## No, I Can't

The fearful mind, trying to protect you, is all about "No." Believing the limited ways in which you define yourself, you focus on thoughts that tell you what you can't do and what's not possible for you. Before you even seriously consider a new idea or direction, your mind tells you all the reasons why it won't work out. You meet any potential that excites you with: *I'll fail. I won't know how to do it. It's too big for me.*

It helps a lot to discover the ways your mind says "No." Reflect on what thoughts are triggered when you start to move outside your comfort zone. When you find the no, feel the contraction into separation and disappointment, and meet these feelings with love and care. The mind is only trying to protect you.

Then practice saying "Yes." It might feel like you're entering a foreign land—the land of yes. *Yes, I can deal with this. Yes, I can give it a shot. Yes, I can find peace here. Yes, I can fully open to the wonder of this moment.*

"No" keeps you stuck in programmed patterns. "Yes" is the nature of consciousness, free of conditioning, welcoming everything as it is.

## Self-Doubt

Someone's comment on my blog captures the pain of self-doubt:

> I live in a constant state of self-doubt and believing that what I truly want cannot be achieved. It's a constant battle in my head that I believe comes from fear. Fear of rejection, of being forgotten, of never being loved again, or that I will fail. I've read countless books and they say this is rumination. I'm always kicking my own @$s. I'm always thinking that if I do this or do that I will be happy. But nothing works.

Self-doubt is paralyzing. It makes you go back and forth endlessly with all the possible options, afraid to make a move. What if you're wrong? What if it doesn't work? What if it does?

Just like with all thoughts that are fear-driven, the content of self-doubting thoughts just isn't true. And if you stay focused on them, you'll be stuck forever. Should you or shouldn't you? You will never answer that question in your thoughts.

The path through self-doubt to peace is to free your attention from these anxious thoughts and welcome the sensations of fear. You're now available to experience the life that's here right in this very moment, liberated from mental concepts. What *should* you do? Float the question, and listen deeply to what comes.

## Dread

One day I realized that I woke up every morning with a pervasive feeling of dread. It had been happening for what seemed like forever before I noticed. As soon as I opened my eyes, I felt heaviness in my chest, and I was afraid of what the day would bring before I even got going. This feeling told me that whatever happened, it would probably be disappointing or upsetting.

When we live under the spell of unworthiness, life can feel heavy as we view every situation through a lens of limitation. It's like trying to function with a dark cloud of negativity hanging over our heads. Noticing and meeting this sense of dread begins to shift your relationship to it. Instead of wishing it weren't present, greet it with a friendly hello.

Once I began to notice this, I breathed with the physical sensations in my body for a few minutes and went on with my day. After some time, I realized that the dread had disappeared, but in truth, it didn't matter. By changing my relationship to it, I was already free.

This is the possibility for all of us.

Reflect on how fear affects your thinking. Take out four blank pages. On the first one write, "How I Worry," on the second, "How I Say 'No, I Can't,'" on the third, "How I Doubt Myself," and on the fourth, "How I Experience Dread."

Turn toward your inner experience, and write as much as you'd like about the topic on each page, adding pages as needed.

Take a few of the statements you've written that you think are true about yourself and bring to them the understanding of the guiding principles and the wisdom of the core practices listed in the appendix. Keep returning your attention to the pure field of awareness. Notice that within that field you're free because it's empty of any personal concerns or limiting ways of thinking about yourself.

# The Sacred Return from Fear

Fear is an integral part of identifying yourself as broken and inadequate. Captured by fear, your body is in "fight or flight" mode and your mind spins with negative thoughts that will never bring you peace. When your attention is entangled in fear-infused thoughts, trying to know what cannot be known, you're missing the beautiful experience of the aliveness that's here and now.

Fearful thoughts guess or assume the worst with no logical evidence. Can you see how fear doesn't want you to be relaxed and happy? It doesn't want you to be comfortable with the unknown or to flourish beyond your mind-created limits. It wants to keep you alert to any worst-case scenarios so that you can keep yourself safe. And who is this "you" we're speaking of? It's the sense of a separate self. It's the one who thinks she is limited by a body and the one who believes that the thoughts that run through her mind define her.

Beyond the limits of these mental concepts that make up the separate identity is the infinite field of consciousness that is untouched by fears about survival and the need to protect. It's pure being that just is—stable, always here, and ever present. When you know the reality of consciousness as your true home, fears—of being found out as the broken one you believe yourself to be, of being less than perfect—lose their power to disturb you.

When it comes to fear, the most liberating statement you can make is "I don't know." "I don't know if I'll find a job." "I don't know if I'll always be alone."

"I don't know" breaks the allegiance to fearful thoughts. It's a truth that uses the mind to align your whole being with the timeless and formless nature of reality. And it opens the door to unlimited possibilities that the frightened mind can't begin to contemplate.

Lose interest in the imagined, scary future, and things will begin to look and feel very different to you. You're not concerned with how you look or worried about being rejected. With the mind no longer occupied by fearful thoughts that close you down, your attention and energy are naturally free, leaving you available to flow with the freshness of the moment. Without the limitations of fear, you're open to appreciation, enjoyment, relaxation, connection, and wonder. New and creative ideas have space to flourish.

Miraculously, you realize that these experiences were always available, but they were masked by the overwhelming power of the fearful mind. Know that fear is likely to arise again because it is built into the wiring of the human nervous system, but stay steady as awareness and it will continue to lose its grip.

No thought defines who you are. Rest your attention in awareness so you can't pretend that the thoughts and feelings that arise are real. Finally seeing through the trance of separation, the world is no longer filled with danger. Everything is you, so you meet what comes with clear seeing and an open heart.

This shift from fear to openness, from division to nonseparation, has practical implications for everyday life. When you awaken to the reality of universal presence, there's a natural outflow unimpeded by fear.

- Ron, who had bolted out of fear whenever anyone around him experienced emotions, became able to listen deeply when his partner expressed herself.

- Madeline, who catered to her friends out of fear of feeling unwanted, began to stay connected to her own creative impulses and love of adventure.

- Lucy, who had isolated herself from others because she felt like she didn't matter, acted on her desire to volunteer her time with children.

As you step out of the familiar shell of lack and limitation, contemplate what actions you can take that arise naturally from generosity, love, and openness. These are actions with no agenda and no goal. You can't think your way to them. They arise as an expression of presence beyond the mind, and by their nature, they're benevolent toward everyone and everything. Let yourself not know anything and be surprised by what appears.

Here are some questions for you to contemplate. You can write your responses in a journal or sit quietly as you reflect on them.

ೀ What negative outcomes or results do you assume will happen? Experiment with saying "I don't know what will happen." Take your time and feel the experience of not knowing in your mind and body.

ೀ What natural impulses or movements want to be expressed in you that you've been suppressing? What actions would you be willing to take to express them?

ೀ What would it be like to embody peace, openness, and enthusiasm for what is appearing in the moment?

ೀ Try this: close your eyes, and then open them as if you're seeing whatever is in front of you for the first time, with no memory or history.

## Living the Awakened Life

Waking up out of the trance of separation and the belief that we're limited by what our minds tell us reveals our true nature, unlimited by any concepts. We're not pulled into the past or future, so we're available to be fully conscious of the all-encompassing timeless presence of this now moment.

This is a radical shift. In one sense, nothing changes. You look in the mirror and see the same face you've always seen. You know how to find the kitchen and prepare something to eat. You drive your children to school without getting lost.

But the old familiar sense of separation is gone. The mind is more spacious as you realize that it functions primarily when it needs to. You're not pulled into self-doubt and sad feelings about yourself. There's no need for the personal self that tries to figure everything out. And you don't rely on your emotions as a benchmark for how things are going. Can you feel the freedom in this way of being?

There's no expectation about what should or shouldn't arise. You experience a reaction that brings hurt, anger, or grief, and it's welcomed fully. You might be grabbed by an old conditioned thought pattern, but quickly you see that it's not you. You know that the thoughts are distorted, limited, and false, and don't define the fullness of you. And you know that you can leave the content of the thoughts and open deeply to feelings. This is how the guiding principles bring clarity to the moment and the core practices support the sacred return to this infinite aliveness.

With great willingness to resist nothing, meeting your experience with awareness and love becomes a joyful undertaking and a lifestyle infused with peace. That's how it's been for me. Fears still arise and my mind can certainly ruminate on self-critical thoughts, but the unhappiness is a signal to wake up to the truth of things—over and over and over. I absolutely know that this peace is already here, outside of the content of any thoughts.

The principles and practices offer the essential foundation needed for the sacred return to consciousness beyond any personal identity. But conditioning can be powerful, and other pointers, detailed below, may help. See which ones resonate with you. Try them out, and let them do their work in you until they naturally fall away, no longer needed.

## The Art of Asking Questions

If a conditioned identity has grabbed you and you feel stuck, one thing you can do is start asking questions. Asking questions is like a healing balm for unhappiness. If you're unhappy, you're believing the contents of the mind. Pose questions, and immediately you're wondering rather than knowing.

Inquiring into your in-the-moment experience is easy because you don't need to know the answer. This isn't a test where you'll be graded on the number of answers you got right. Instead, discover the space of consciousness that is receptive, open, and curious. Simply float the questions through your mind, and notice what arises.

Sit quietly and take a few conscious breaths. Then introduce any of these questions. Read them slowly, pausing after each one.

- What is most alive in me right now?

- What can I surrender right now that isn't serving?

- What false beliefs am I taking to be true?

- What am I avoiding that is asking for my attention?

- Can I say "Yes!" to what's happening right now?

- Can I welcome what's happening in my body right now?

- What is life asking of me?

- Can I stop, breathe, and simply be aware?

- Who or what am I?

- Can I open to what is here right now?

- Where is my attention going? Is this supporting peace?

- How can I be more aligned with what I really want?

- What would love do if I didn't let fear drive me?

- How does life want to move me right now, beyond fear?

- How can I bring kindness to this moment?

- How can I bring ease to my experience in this moment?

Asking questions is a path to a deeply felt conscious life free of conditioning. It breaks through programmed patterns and creates space for insights to come, uncaused by you, from the true knowing beyond the mind.

## Tap Into the Inner Coach

Most thinking pulls your attention away from presence and into division created by the mind. But sometimes thoughts can support the return to openness and peace.

For a while, a phrase that popped into my mind when I was experiencing emotions was "Go in." To me, that meant to shift attention out of thoughts and into the sensations present in the body. Repeating this phrase helped me tremendously to unravel my connection to thought and to simply open with awareness to physical sensations. Eventually the sensations themselves were seen to have no reference to a personal "me." And when the phrase was no longer needed, it stopped appearing.

One client's phrase is "Go back." To her it means to lose interest in objects and make the sacred return out of the personal identity and into conscious awareness. Someone else says "Let go" when she realizes her attention has been glued to spinning thoughts. And a friend replaces "Not this!" with "Oh, this," which ends drama and invites a deep allowing of things as they are.

Now it's your turn. Is there an inner coach wanting to steer you toward the deepest truth? See if there is a helpful phrase that arises naturally in support of awakening from the spell of unworthiness. If nothing appears, let this practice go and see what other forms of guidance spark your interest.

## Surrender

"Surrender" means to give up. If you want to know the endless peace that's possible, be willing to give up everything you believe to be true. With surrender, you leave the world of your limited identity and open to the sacred space of aliveness that is infinitely greater than you.

Imagine bundling up everything personal to you in a lovely gilded box. What do you put into the box? Fears, expectations, judgments, memories, self-criticisms, and ideas about what is and isn't okay. Add in your familiar life stories and their associated emotions. Honor all of these things for their attempts to help you function—and realize the wisdom of removing them as the filter through which you view yourself and the world.

Put the box away in safe storage as you surrender everything to do with your personal self. Where does that leave you? Here, with no division between you and the world. And what do you notice? Naturally arising compassion and understanding of others' suffering...a heart that's generous without needing anything back...a reliable sense of trust in the unfolding of life...deep stillness that brings about a relaxed way of being in the world...the quiet voice of inner knowing...

Now bring the box back and open the lid. You can reactivate the personal filter of emotions, defenses, identities, and needs—or rest consciously as the clear, open space of aware presence. Which appeals to you?

Surrender is available to you in any moment. Whatever you're holding on to, give it back, drop the weight, and trust that things will be okay.

- If you're going back and forth in your mind trying to make a decision, surrender the effort and listen.

- If you feel confused and off track, surrender the need to know.

- If you're caught in an old pattern of self-judgment, surrender that inner voice as a definition of who you are.

It's possible to get very good at surrender. Whenever you catch yourself in a moment of personal suffering, you always have the option to do a reset. Surrender the belief in your thoughts. Surrender the need to analyze your feelings. Simplify everything by giving up all effort and here you are, peaceful.

## Remembering the Body

I've mentioned the usefulness of opening to sensations in the body, and this deserves repeating. The body is a gateway into presence. We often ignore the experiences that appear in the body while our attention is gripped by the mind. Opening to physical sensations directs our attention away from the thinking mind and into the reality of the moment.

And unmet sensations are at the root of the separate self. Allowing these to be present without any story attached short-circuits the contraction that makes you believe you're separate.

Being fully with sensations means that you're not resisting any experience. Rather, you're in harmony with what's here. Be so harmonious with your present-moment experience that all division falls away. Deeply welcome these sensations so much that they dissolve into awareness.

There is so much wisdom in the body. Opening to sensations with no agenda invites you to learn the language the body speaks. If you allow a great space for the reactions of the body, a whole world opens up. You notice subtle changes in heart rate, breathing, muscular tension, and digestion. You feel tightness, softness, vibration, heaviness, empty space. There are urges to react—the residue of emotions that have been buried outside of conscious awareness— and an inner knowing that doesn't come from the thinking mind. Be very open to what the body has to say.

Let awareness of the body expand into the space around it. Especially with your eyes closed, you'll notice sensations appearing and disappearing, but they're not contained within the object you call your body. Expanding your exploration beyond the outline of the body gives an offering of free space for sensations to unfold naturally with no expectations.

## Turn Toward Qualities of Awakened Awareness

The awakened life embodies qualities that are freely expressed, once attention is unhooked from contracted thinking. These are qualities familiar to all of us, but we overlook them when we're bound by our conditioning.

Why not consciously turn toward these already existing manifestations of awakened awareness? You know them as moments of unbridled joy, free-flowing heart connections with no barriers, laughing uncontrollably, or being immersed in the flow of an enjoyable experience. In these moments, although we may not notice it, the commentary of the mind stops and we experience ourselves as inseparable from whatever is arising. There is just the all-encompassing reality of what's here, and no separate person who is doing anything or making anything happen. All conditioning falls away, and there is direct experiencing of the expressions of pure consciousness. It's a delightful way to live!

Conditioned thoughts and feelings are temporary—they appear and disappear. Keep abandoning these temporary appearances, because they are the source of personal suffering. Turn your attention to the here-and-now experiences of peace, joy, tenderness, gratitude, and happiness. What you allow is what grows.

# The Fire for Awakening

As we conclude our journey together, how do you move forward from here? How do you continue to embody the understanding that you are not the one who is inadequate and broken?

First, from my full heart, I want to congratulate you. I honor you for the journey you've chosen to take and for your heartfelt willingness to courageously investigate the ways you suffer so you can discover the deepest truth about yourself. You now know that the beliefs telling you that you're unworthy and that you don't matter don't define the brilliance of who you are. You are luminous, empty of form, and overflowing with life. You don't need to add a single thing that isn't already here to be the magnificence that you are. It's your natural self.

The reality of your true nature as loving awareness is always the case and here to be known. And the patterns that have defined you for so long are sticky—they will recur, so be prepared.

Once you notice the slightest bit of suffering, discover the wisdom that the guiding principles bring to your experience and begin to walk through the core practices. Keep resting your attention in consciousness beyond any objects. And rinse and repeat as often as necessary. Let this way of being with your experience become a lifestyle that you enjoy and appreciate. Relish being fully alive to what's here in the moment!

Contemplate the power of making a commitment to the freedom you really want. This power became apparent to my friend Angela in an unlikely circumstance. Much to her surprise, grieving the loss of her beloved dog sparked a tremendous natural uprising of kindness that began to permeate every area of her life. It's the type of kindness that comes from pure empathy, the recognition of the one heart that dissolves all separation. She glowed as she shared with me her dedication to allowing this newfound realization of kindness to transform her whole way of being. It was a beautiful movement beyond her contracted, separate self.

A strong commitment stokes the inner fire like nothing else. We stop pretending that our true desire doesn't matter, and we devote ourselves entirely to it. If your true desire is to be free of the suffering that unworthiness brings to your life, then commit to finding your way through in any moment.

When we commit, we close the door to the known and step into endless possibilities. We shift from going through the motions like an automaton to intelligence, wisdom, and alignment. What do we commit to?

- Being conscious in the moments of our lives;

- Choosing skillfully;

- Investigating how we turn away; and

- Returning to boundless peace over and over.

Commit fully to who you are beyond all stories, and see what wonders are set in motion in your precious life.

# ACKNOWLEDGMENTS

Bowing down with deepest gratitude to all my teachers who have illuminated the way.

I'm grateful for the wholehearted support of the staff at New Harbinger Publications for helping this book come to fruition and for giving me the opportunity to share this most important message—that suffering is truly optional.

With special thanks to Judy Paulino and Craig Sorensen for their reading of the manuscript, to Melissa Valentine for her enthusiastic support of my work, to Nancy and Gene Krug for their friendship and love, and to Arielle Ela-Ra and Marlon Jeffers for the gift of time to write.

Finally, I wish to acknowledge the courage and commitment of the people I've worked with over the years, who have shared their struggles in their desire to be free. Their paths inspire the awakening of all.

# FOUR GUIDING PRINCIPLES AND FIVE CORE PRACTICES

## Guiding Principles

1. The identity of "I am not enough" is made up of distorted thoughts that view the self, others, and the world through a lens that is limited and false.

2. No matter how real it seems, the identity of unworthiness is optional. You don't *have to* be defined by it.

3. You have control over shifting your attention to different parts of your experience.

4. There is more to your experience in any moment than your thoughts and feelings.

# Core Practices

1. Turning toward your experience

2. The safe haven of being aware

3. Losing interest in thoughts

4. Welcoming feelings

5. The sacred return

# REFERENCES

Ainsworth, M., M. Blehar, E. Waters, and S. Wall. 1978. *Patterns of Attachment: A Psychological Study of the Strange Situation.* Hillsdale, NJ: Lawrence Erlbaum.

Bowlby, J. 1988. *A Secure Base: Parent-Child Attachment and Healthy Human Development.* London: Routledge.

Darwin, C. 1859. *On the Origin of Species by Means of Natural Selection, or, the Preservation of Favoured Races in the Struggle for Life.* London: J. Murray.

Nisargadatta Maharaj. 2012. *I Am That* Rev. ed. Durham, NC: Acorn Press.

Spira, R. 2016a. *The Ashes of Love: Sayings on the Essence of Non-Duality.* Oxford: Sahaja.

Spira, R. 2016b. *The Transparency of Things: Contemplating the Nature of Experience* 2nd ed. Oxford: Sahaja.

Tolle, E. 2005. *A New Earth.* London: Penguin.

**Gail Brenner, PhD,** is a clinical psychologist who joyfully helps people discover that suffering is optional. Through investigating her own experience and working with clients for over twenty-five years, she has discovered how to unravel common problems of everyday life to reveal the deepest acceptance and peace. Author of the award-winning *The End of Self-Help* and *At the Core of Every Heart*, she lives in Santa Barbara, CA. To learn more, please visit www.gailbrenner.com.

Foreword writer **Rick Archer** learned meditation in 1968 and has been practicing it a couple of hours a day without fail since then. He also taught meditation for twenty-five years. Rick created *Buddha at the Gas Pump* in the fall of 2009 and has since interviewed 250 "spiritually awakening" people, from the well-known to the unknown, and from a variety of backgrounds and traditions. He conducts a new interview each week. Rick has a master's degree in the science of creative intelligence (Vedic studies) from Maharishi University of Management. He lives in Iowa with his wife Irene and their two dogs.

# MORE BOOKS for the SPIRITUAL SEEKER

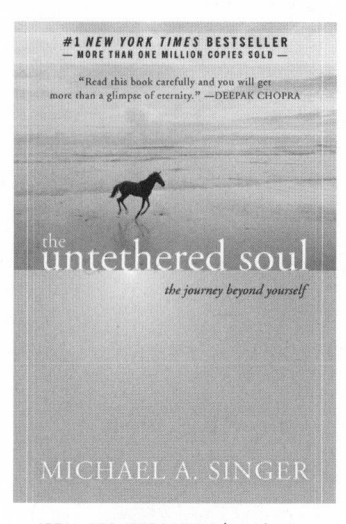

Register your **new harbinger** titles for additional benefits!

When you register your **new harbinger** title—purchased in any format, from any source—you get access to benefits like the following:

- Downloadable accessories like printable worksheets and extra content

- Instructional videos and audio files

- Information about updates, corrections, and new editions

Not every title has accessories, but we're adding new material all the time.

Access free accessories in 3 easy steps:

1. Sign in at NewHarbinger.com (or **register** to create an account).

2. Click on **register a book**. Search for your title and click the **register** button when it appears.

3. Click on the **book cover or title** to go to its details page. Click on **accessories** to view and access files.

That's all there is to it!

If you need help, visit:

NewHarbinger.com/accessories

**new harbinger**
CELEBRATING
**40** YEARS